GOD'S CONSTANT PRESENCE

True Stories of Everyday Miracles

Beloved *by* His Faithful

GOD'S CONSTANT PRESENCE
True Stories of Everyday Miracles

Beloved *by* His Faithful

EDITORS OF GUIDEPOSTS

Guideposts

A Gift from Guideposts

Thank you for your purchase! We appreciate your support and want to express our gratitude with a special gift just for you.

Dive into *Spirit Lifters*, a complimentary booklet that will fortify your faith and offer solace during challenging moments. It contains 31 carefully selected verses from scripture that will soothe your soul and uplift your spirit.

Please use the QR code or go to **guideposts.org/spiritlifters** to download.

Beloved by His Faithful

Published by Guideposts
100 Reserve Road, Suite E200
Danbury, CT 06810
Guideposts.org

Copyright © 2025 by Guideposts. All rights reserved.

This book, or parts thereof, may not be reproduced, stored in a retrieval system, or transmitted in any form or by any means, electronic, mechanical, photocopying, recording or otherwise, without the written permission of the publisher.

Cover design by Serena Fox Design Company
Interior design by Serena Fox Design Company
Cover photo Shot Fotos
Typeset by Aptara, Inc.

ISBN 978-1-961442-24-5 (hardcover)
ISBN 978-1-961442-25-2 (softcover)
ISBN 978-1-961442-26-9 (epub)

Printed and bound in the United States of America

Therefore if you have any encouragement from being united with Christ, if any comfort from his love, if any common sharing in the Spirit, if any tenderness and compassion, then make my joy complete by being like-minded, having the same love, being one in spirit and of one mind. . . . In humility value others above yourselves, not looking to your own interests but each of you to the interests of the others.

—Philippians 2:1–4 (NIV)

TABLE *of* CONTENTS

Introduction........................1
    Who Loves Ya, Baby?

Chapter 1..........................7
    God Sends His Helpers

Chapter 2.........................41
    Guided to Bless Others

Chapter 3.........................81
    Blessings of Friends and Family

Chapter 4........................115
    Connected at the Right Time

Chapter 5........................149
    Community of Caring

Chapter 6........................199
    God Speaks through Others

Contributors 229

Acknowledgments 230

Who Loves Ya, Baby?

Jeanette Levellie

FROM 1973 TO 1978, the late actor Telly Savalas played a hard-bitten NYC cop on the hit TV series *Kojak*. The character's favorite saying was, "Who loves ya, baby?" That phrase might be passé now, but it's a question we often ask ourselves when tragedy strikes, we have a complicated problem, or we merely need encouragement. The obvious answer is "God loves me." But how does God best show His love for us?

Through other people of faith.

It started with Jesus, this idea of proving God's love by helping others. Jesus then passed it down to His followers. We, like Jesus, are motivated by compassion and kindness. We, like Jesus, love to comfort and encourage. We, like Jesus, gain the utmost joy from serving others.

The true stories in this book all reflect this selfless, Jesus-like service. Whether accounts of helping someone out of danger or merely giving a word of cheer to a sagging soul, these stories will give you a fresh sense of wonder at grace given from one individual to another, or from a community to a person in need. And perhaps they will also give you a few ideas of ways to show Jesus's love to your neighbor.

So when someone asks you, "Who loves ya, baby?" you'll answer, "God, through Jesus Christ. Because His followers love so well."

Help Is on the Way

WHEN WE'RE IN trouble, we need a rescuer. The trouble can be anything from a lost kitten to a mountain of debt to a hurricane that washed away our entire town.

My husband Kevin, a pastor, once rescued a church member from committing suicide. It was our anniversary. We'd returned home from a lovely dinner out and had just settled on the sofa to watch a romantic movie when the ringing phone interrupted our plan. After answering, Kev listened for a few seconds and then grabbed his still-warm jacket. As he rushed out he said, "Pray! Lenny is threatening to kill himself and the police want me there."

Lenny was a new member of our congregation. His wife had recently left him, taking their two kids with her.

I later learned from Kevin that when he arrived at Lenny's apartment complex, flashing red lights from a dozen police cars illumined the white stucco on nearby buildings. The inebriated Lenny was in his kitchen waving a butcher knife and shouting. Kevin approached the doorway and prayed God would put words in his mouth to help Lenny. After 45 minutes of calm talking, Kevin asked for the knife. Lenny handed it to him with shaking hands and then slumped into a kitchen chair. "Everyone there sighed in relief when Lenny let the police lead him to their squad car to take him to the hospital for help," Kev told me.

When my husband walked through our front door several hours later, he too slumped into a kitchen chair. After hearing Lenny's story, I think I must have been the second-most relieved woman on earth. After Lenny's mom.

I can almost hear God applauding every time Kevin and I talk about that story. Just as I believe He applauded the Apostle Paul for the same type of rescue in the prison at Phillipi:

About midnight Paul and Silas were praying and singing hymns to God, and the other prisoners were listening to them. Suddenly there was such a violent earthquake that the foundations of the prison were shaken. At once all the prison doors flew open, and everyone's chains came loose. The jailer woke up, and when he saw the prison doors open, he drew his sword and was about to kill himself because he thought the prisoners had escaped. But Paul shouted, "Don't harm yourself! We are all here!"

The jailer called for lights, rushed in and fell trembling before Paul and Silas. He then brought them out and asked, "Sirs, what must I do to be saved?" (Acts 16:25–30, NIV)

Paul and Silas could have simply left the prison. They'd been treated unfairly by the authorities, and they had no obligation to the jailer. But they put the jailer's life before their own safety, and in the end not only were they released, but the jailer became a Christian because of the divine love they'd demonstrated.

Whether we save a life or merely inspire a sigh of relief, whenever we rescue someone we bring God's presence.

Pistachio Pudding

LYDIA WAS A former member of a church Kevin pastored in California. Her husband, Bud, had suffered a stroke that left him debilitated in several ways. Lydia refused to place Bud in a nursing facility. She cared for Bud at home. In spite of her limited income, Lydia rented a hospital bed and had it placed in the living room where Bud could view the Southern California palm trees and cloudless skies from their sparkling picture window. Lydia came every time Bud called, fed him, and kept their TV—loud—on his favorite channel.

Bud was not the sweetest plum on the tree before his stroke. Afterward, he became more demanding and selfish than ever. Oh, did I mention that Bud lost his ability to speak? The best he could do was a garbled groan that got louder and angrier the longer he had to wait for Lydia to bring an extra blanket or make his pistachio pudding.

One day when Kevin and I visited Lydia and Bud, he began shouting unintelligibly as soon as we sat down on the couch next to his bed. "It's OK, Bud," Lydia said. "They aren't going to stay long." I could feel my eyebrows jump as I glanced sideways at Kevin. Unfortunately, Lydia noticed. "He doesn't like when people visit," she explained. "He wants all my attention for himself." She walked over to the hospital bed, held Bud's hand gently in her own, and spoke to him in a calming tone. "You're my sweet baby, aren't you, honey?"

When we got in the car I asked Kevin how long Lydia and Bud were married. "Over 40 years," he said. He shook his head. "I marvel at her devotion to him." She personified the Apostle Paul's instruction, "Whatever you do, work at it with all your heart, as working for the Lord, not for human masters" (Colossians 3:23, NIV).

At Bud's funeral the following year, Lydia stood by his casket and sobbed. "Oh, why did he have to die, Lord? Why? Why? Why?" I was stunned. Bud's death wasn't a relief to Lydia? She wished for more time to care for him, no matter how demanding he acted? Although I'd been following Jesus since I was a child, in that moment I received a revelation. Lydia's commitment to Bud reflected God's constant care for His children. Thankless though we are, He runs when we call, holds our hand, and brings us pudding.

The Best Encourager

DURING THE ANNOUNCEMENT time at a weight loss meeting I attended several years ago, the voice of the president, Sally, faltered. "Darlene is discouraged today. She asked that if anyone has a kind word or a hug for her, she'll appreciate it."

Wow, I thought as I halfheartedly listened to the rest of the meeting. *What a novel idea simply to ask for encouragement from people we trust. I need to do that when I'm feeling down.* When the gathering ended, all seventeen of us lined up to embrace Darlene, tell her how much they admired her, and say that God was on her side.

Since that day, I've reached out to a couple of my closest friends for words of grace when I feel downhearted. It works! My friends always come through with kind words, proving that we're family. We need to "think about each other to see how we can encourage each other" (Hebrews 10:24, ERV).

But the one who gives me the best encouragement is God. When my mood sinks lower than a snake's belly in a Texas rut, I ask my Father for help: "Dear Lord, please send me a friend, a song, a prayer, or a Bible verse to help me through this dark tunnel of hopelessness." And because God is love and kindness itself, He never fails to lift me up out of my discouragement. I'll hear the perfect song in the car, receive a "You made my day" card in the mail, or a usually less-than-effusive friend will compliment me.

My prayer for you as you read the stories in this volume is that you'll feel tucked inside God's heart, encouraged by His love, and covered by His sweet, constant care.

God wisely gave us each other to make our ways through life. When we help another get back up, our own spirits resurrect.

—Farrell Mason

CHAPTER 1

God Sends His Helpers

Comfort from a Friend 8
    Mindy Baker

Roadside Rescue 12
    Heather Jepsen

He Cares for My Heart. 16
    Kristen Paris

Ambassadors of Hope 22
    Elizabeth Erlandson

Can't Claim Coincidence 26
    Laura Bailey

God Did That. 30
    Tracy Ruckman

More Than a Mountain Hike 35
    Constance B. Fink

Comfort from a Friend

Mindy Baker

A few years ago, we started noticing a change in my dad. He had become very withdrawn and apathetic, sleeping many hours a day. Before he had always been a people person who enjoyed having friends over to socialize or to welcome the church's newcomers by visiting them, but now he had no interest in anything. We began to wonder if he was suffering from depression. I tried to coach him to find a hobby or plan a fun trip to take with Mom to help pull him out of his gloom, but it didn't work. I missed his big grin.

A year later, doctors diagnosed him with Parkinson's disease due to tremors and other symptoms he was experiencing. But over time, the medicines for Parkinson's were not helping. Other symptoms appeared that did not match that diagnosis. He and my mom continued to search for a doctor that could help him.

We could see that the mystery disease was attacking his brain. Over time he began to lose his balance, and he had trouble swallowing and difficulty speaking. Even his vision was affected. His body was slowly shutting down. As the disease progressed, Mom tried to take care of him the best she could, but it became too much. He was consistently falling, and his debilitating symptoms progressed beyond what she could manage. Eventually, he could neither walk nor care for himself and needed full-time assistance in a nursing facility. That is where he finally received the correct diagnosis: progressive supranuclear palsy. Having a diagnosis was helpful, but it didn't solve anything. There was no cure.

It was difficult to watch him continue to spiral downward. In the last few months of his life, he could not feed himself, and he had to have his food pureed and his water thickened so that he wouldn't choke or aspirate. Living 8 hours away, I visited as much as I could, and with each trip I noted the marked decline in his abilities and in his physical appearance. I wondered how much more time he had left with us. Driving home after each visit, I wondered, *Was that the last time I'll see Dad?*

My mom was constantly at his side. She visited each day, showing him Christ-like love. I also came to appreciate individuals like Jammin' Joe, a chaplain who ministered to Dad and the other residents at the nursing home by playing his guitar, singing, talking with them, and praying for them.

> **Perfume and incense bring joy to the heart, and the pleasantness of a friend springs from their heartfelt advice.**
>
> —PROVERBS 27:9 (NIV)

One day, when Mom was visiting Dad, she tripped on a cord near his bedside, hit her head, and had to be rushed to a nearby hospital, where she was diagnosed with a brain injury. Dad was lucid enough to understand what had happened, but that knowledge seemed to trigger a rapid decline in his condition.

A week later, I received a call from one of his nurses. She said that Dad was not eating at all anymore and could no longer swallow any of the thickened water. Because of his DNR order and out of respect for his wishes, all she could do for him was swab his mouth and keep him comfortable with medication. She recommended that I come to say my goodbyes while he would be able to comprehend that I was there and understand my words. I drove to see him.

Meanwhile, my mom was recovering from her fall. She had made it out of the hospital and into a physical rehabilitation facility. When I arrived, my brother and I went and told her the news. We were able to sign her out to go with us to visit Dad for the last time.

In my mind, I have replayed that day and the conversation we had in the room many times. I am glad I was there, and I tried to say the right things, but I wish I had been more eloquent.

Because of my job, I had to return home after the visit. A few days later, I received the phone call telling me that Dad had gone to be with his Savior in heaven. Once again, I loaded up our van—only this time it was to travel to the funeral.

In the midst of my grief, God provided the comfort of friends. There were three specific instances in which I remember feeling very alone and almost paralyzed, unable to do the next thing. And in all three moments, God faithfully prompted a friend to reach out to me with encouragement.

First was a former pastor and his wife that my husband and I had ministered alongside for many years. They called to pray with me before we made the drive to the funeral. "You were a good daughter," the pastor said. I felt the Holy Spirit wrap His arms around me with that comment, because before that call my mind had been filled with all the ways that I had fallen short of being a "good daughter." *How had he known exactly what I needed to hear?*

The second was the morning before the funeral. I was making a memory board from old photos and grief overcame me. I went into the room where I was staying and opened my Bible. All was quiet. At that moment, I received a text message. It was a friend who wanted to know if there was any specific way she could pray for me. She said that God had placed me on her mind. I will never forget the precise timing of that message.

Finally, another friend called me the morning of the funeral. I was on a walk, praying for guidance, wondering if I should try and speak at the funeral. When I saw her name flash onto my phone, I picked up immediately. Hearing her voice melted my heart, and she talked me through my decision.

> **The eternal God is your refuge, and underneath are the everlasting arms.**
>
> —DEUTERONOMY 33:27 (NIV)

In the midst of the loss of my dad, God was there. He saw the needs of my heart and knew what would help me. He provided the sweet comfort from friends to offer me tangible evidence of His presence not just once, but three times. I'm very thankful that my friends responded to God's prompting to call me. I will never forget it.

Roadside Rescue

Heather Jepsen

It was the summer of 1992, when I was a precocious middle schooler. Our family was on a road trip, and as we crossed the vast, sparsely populated regions of eastern Montana, our car began to lurch and struggle. Slowly my father pulled the family van over to the shoulder, parking against a guardrail, and got out to look at the car. Not being much of a mechanic, all he could see under the hood was that we needed help.

Nowadays we would just make a call on our cell phone, but as my kids often remind me, I grew up in the "dark ages" before such modern conveniences. My father stuck his head back in the car, said goodbye to me, my mom, and my brother, and promptly crossed the divided highway on foot.

As we all sat and watched, my father began to walk back towards the most recent town behind us, sticking up his thumb like a character in a movie. It was not long before a stranger stopped and whisked my father away to the great unknown.

As my mother, brother, and I sat in the van, silence began to descend. What were we going to do now? My mother did her best to keep us kids calm and collected. "It's no use panicking," she told us. My little brother got out his Game Boy and started to entertain himself. And me? I started to pray.

We didn't go to church as a family when I was growing up, but that previous summer I had joined a church and been baptized. This was the first time I had really been in need since then, so when I felt afraid, I turned my heart to God. "Dear God, please keep us safe. Please send help," I whispered.

The silence stretched on as we waited, interrupted only by the rushing of semitrucks as they passed our smaller van. As we sat waiting, my mother noticed a semitruck pulling over on our side of the road. He began to slow down and inch his big rig right up behind our car. We all were beside ourselves with fear. Truckers were rumored to be a tough and scary lot, and here we were, a helpless woman and two kids stuck by the side of the road.

When the big rig came to a halt, a grizzled-looking man dropped out of the cab and began to walk toward our car. We were shaking with fear. "Please God please God please God," I prayed, hoping we would be OK.

> **I will say of the L<small>ORD</small>, "He is my refuge and my fortress, my God, in whom I trust."**
>
> —PSALM 91:2 (NIV)

The man knocked on my mom's window and she nervously rolled it down.

"Yes?" she murmured.

"Are you all OK?" he asked in a friendly voice. "Do you need help?"

"I think we are OK," my mom replied. "My husband went back to town to get help."

"Well," he said, "the truckers going the other direction saw you all stopped here, and they radioed to me to check in on you. Everyone on the road wants to make sure you are OK. I will radio out that help is on the way, but if you are still here come an hour from now, I will send help myself."

"Well, thank you, sir. That's very kind of you," my mom replied.

As he walked back to his big rig my brother and I marveled. Maybe truck drivers weren't that scary after all. Here we were, thinking we were all alone in the world, while all the truck drivers speeding past were actually watching over us.

About 30 minutes later, a baby-blue tow truck pulled up behind our car. Out popped the most handsome man my adolescent eyes had ever seen. And along with him was my dad! The driver came to our van and said he was there to tow us to the nearest mechanic.

> "If you believe, you will receive whatever you ask for in prayer."
>
> —MATTHEW 21:22 (NIV)

We all got out and watched as he hooked our car up to the towing system. As he worked, I noticed a huge silver cross around his neck. I knew in my heart it was a sign from God. This man was a Christian and God had sent him to help us. And he was so good-looking, with his dimples and blue eyes, I wondered if maybe God had sent an angel our way.

Once our car was safely connected to the tow truck, all four of us piled into the tow cab with the driver and headed toward town. He dropped us off at a hotel and took the van to be worked on.

I was too young at the time to remember what happened with the car or why it didn't work. But I do remember that this ended up being the best day of our whole vacation. We took a taxi to a mall (my first time in a taxi!) and walked around to look at things, we swam in the hotel pool, and at night my parents let my brother and I order in pizza all by ourselves while they went out to dinner. I felt so grown up as I called the pizza place from the hotel phone to place our order.

The hotel even backed up to a rodeo ground, so my brother and I could watch horseback riding and bucking broncos out

GOD'S GIFT OF SOUND
— Terrie Todd —

FOR MANY, THE slap of hockey sticks on ice, the whack of pucks against boards, and the swoosh of blades zig-zagging down an outdoor rink can elicit fond memories of childhood that evoke joy, nostalgia, and, hopefully, a reminder of God's presence. Kids who grow up with a knowledge of their Creator hear His voice and feel His presence in anything that gives them happiness. What a great gift from God, that even these ordinary sounds can bring a reminder of His presence!

---

of the hotel window as we ate our pepperoni pizza. Now in our 40s, he and I both remember this as one of the best times that we have ever shared together.

As an adult I realize how formative this experience was for me. When I needed help, God sent it. How different would my faith journey have been if bad things had happened that day! But the semitruck driver was a reminder that help can come from surprising sources. And the tow truck driver's cross was a clear sign of the presence of God in my midst. For a young person, receiving such a clear answer to prayer instilled in me such confidence. I knew God was with me, I knew prayers were answered, and I knew I would never be alone.

I learned on that day that when I am afraid, when I need protection and hope, I can turn to God in prayer. God always sends surprising things my way. While it doesn't always turn out as well as pizza and a rodeo from a hotel window, I am never alone when I seek the protection of God.

He Cares for My Heart

Kristen Paris

I gazed out the window as the first pink streaks of dawn awakened the forest, stirring my heart with its dewy beauty and beckoning me outside. Meandering between the Ponderosa pines, I thanked God for the privilege of living in this peaceful sanctuary. Yet, in the extreme stillness, a vague loneliness nagged at my heart.

Living in Black Forest, Colorado, was a dream come true. Our 5-acre parcel of trees felt worlds away from the nearby city of Colorado Springs, offering me the opportunity to homeschool our children in natural serenity without unwanted interruptions. The joy of having a natural science lab and physical education field as our own backyard was never lost on me. But something was missing—companionship.

Homeschool moms have little social time. It's a 24/7 job that sometimes feels like more. Generally, I didn't mind. I'd committed to it, and I wouldn't have traded that choice for the world. But at times, it would have been nice to hear the voice of someone over the age of eight. Someone for whom I wasn't responsible.

My husband spent most of his weekdays out of town on business. We talked on the phone nightly, and he heard all about the kids' happenings, praying with them from afar. But the days were long and tiring, and I was beginning to feel a bit too isolated.

Our children had friends from their myriad of activities, but nobody near enough to just run over and play with. My time was so engulfed by the duties of homeschooling that even when they were at functions or play dates, I was usually busy grading papers, picking up library books, or grocery shopping. I longed for someone close by for the quick, scattered moments—another woman to share the ups and downs with.

I sighed and went back inside to wake my little ones and get started on another day of reading, writing, and arithmetic. Was it selfish for me to have needs? It felt that way. My life was about the kids now. But that night, I prayed to find friendship in the forest. I didn't know how, but I knew that God could meet this need, as He had so many others, or make me content to live without.

One lot away from our home, a small cul-de-sac branched off to the east. I rarely noticed it. But one day as we were passing by, a sign caught my eye: "House for Sale." It was only the second time I'd seen a house in our area for sale in the 8 years we had lived there. I blinked, half expecting the sign to disappear.

> **You keep track of all my sorrows. You have collected all my tears in your bottle. You have recorded each one in your book.**
>
> —PSALM 56:8 (NLT)

Christian friends of ours who also homeschooled their children were looking for a new home, and they were considering our area. This was perfect! I called them as soon as we pulled into our driveway. I could finally have a sister in Christ nearby. I was so excited.

Our friends called the realtor.

"Sorry, that house sold yesterday."

My joyful bubble burst.

No, no, no, no, no! My heart cried in near despair. I wanted a friend close by so badly. How could God let me get my hopes up, then crush them so soon?

I shared my frustration with my husband, but he didn't fully understand. Of course he wouldn't. He was with people all the time at work and loved coming home to quiet and solitude. "Has it occurred to you that maybe God wants you to be the one to introduce someone new to Him?" he questioned softly, meaning to encourage me to adopt a more optimistic perspective.

Sure, I grumbled inwardly. It occurred to me. I just didn't like it.

Didn't my loneliness matter to God? I taught all day, every day, training our children to know God. I worked in a Bible study group for children and Sunday school, representing Christ to other people's children. That was my entire life. But where was my opportunity to soak in Christian fellowship without the responsibility of being in charge, of being the giver? Where could I go when I was hurt, confused, or just weighed down with daily life?

That night, I prayed my desperation out on my pillow as silent tears rolled down my face. The emptiness of being too often alone, confused, and feeling inadequate to tackle the many challenges of homeschooling ate away at my soul. God was enough, of course, but He also made me for community. Finally, with a semi-resigned sigh, I gave it one more try.

"God, please, couldn't You make the new neighbors Christians with children somewhat close in age to our own? I know the house already sold, but You also already knew I'd be praying this prayer, so maybe could You answer in the past somehow? Lord, I love You, and I love the life You've given me, but I am so lonely. Please see my heart."

Sharing my prayer the next morning with my husband threw me right back into frustration mode.

"Might that be a bit selfish?" he suggested. "Why not just pray that God will use you in their lives, whoever they may be? Think of the blessing you could be to them."

Hmph, I pouted inwardly. *Fine. I'll just go on alone.*

The new neighbors moved in, and I was too disappointed to think about meeting strangers I was sure I wouldn't like. They got the house I wanted our friends to have, and in my opinion, they didn't belong there!

Months later, our daughters were practicing archery with their dad in our backyard range, which ran along the fence line between our property and the new neighbors—the only area we'd cleared of trees. It turned out to be a play day for our neighbors as well, and over our fence, my husband finally made the contact I should have made weeks earlier.

> **Cast all your anxiety on him because he cares for you.**
>
> —1 PETER 5:7 (NIV)

It was my husband's birthday that day, but finances were tight, so we were celebrating with a simple spaghetti dinner and a grocery-store cake from the shelf of baked goods about to expire. It was definitely not a meal worthy of company. But that evening, our new neighbors joined us in our uncleaned, lived-in, cramped dining room littered with schoolbooks and projects.

Over a meal seasoned with laughter, we learned that they were a Christian family with two delightful children just a few years older than our own oldest daughter. They'd even begun attending our church. And as icing on the cake, they homeschooled.

The girls became instant friends, as did their mom and I. Before long, my husband installed a gate in the fence between our lots so we could run back and forth easily. That gate has seen nearly daily use for more than two decades now.

God had answered my prayer before I had even uttered it. What a wonderful, loving, wise Father He is! The shame I felt for not having trusted in His care—and also for not having bothered to go meet the new neighbors at the first opportunity—was washed away by my delight. My new friend had been going through her own struggles, having been uprooted and moved to a state she hadn't wanted to come to. She'd been pouting inwardly too!

We both learned to trust Him more deeply for the little everyday needs beyond the physical basics.

That friendship grew into annual sledding days celebrating each year's first big snow, German lessons together, tea parties, swim team carpools, Christmas season walks through the woods by lantern light to gather around cream puffs filled with peppermint ice cream and chocolate sauce, and so much more.

We walked through the homeschool years knowing we always had a listening ear, arm to lean on, and shoulder to cry on.

Together, we navigated the grief of losing our homes in the Black Forest wildfires. Side by side, we rebuilt. Each of us propped the other up when our husbands went through serious medical issues. We grieved together at the loss of loved ones.

But at the start of that friendship, God had more up His sleeve.

About a year later, the house two doors up the street went up for sale. It didn't seem right to ask for another such blessing.

But, almost ashamed to do so, I whispered another tentative prayer.

And God answered again. Another Christian homeschool family, with girls close to the ages of our own and a son slightly younger than ours established themselves two doors away. Their girls danced, as did our second daughter. Our children participated in drama productions together, and more friendships flourished.

But wait, there's more! God must have laughed in delight as He showered blessings on us again. Shortly thereafter, the house next door to us went up for sale. Hesitantly, I prayed again, pretty sure I was asking too much, and content if God answered no.

Christian homeschool family number three moved in, with boys close to our children's ages! When their mom was called to jury duty, my homeschool table expanded to include the neighbor boys. When we had financial struggles, they showed up at our door with bags of groceries. They were later blessed with two girls, and when those daughters took an interest in ballet, our second daughter became their first teacher.

> **In every situation, by prayer and petition, with thanksgiving, present your requests to God.**
>
> —PHILIPPIANS 4:6 (NIV)

Loneliness had vanished like mist in the sunshine. Four homeschool houses in a row is practically unheard of, particularly in our sparsely populated area. It's too unusual to be random chance.

Only God, with tender love, could bring this about.

He truly does care for my heart. And He cares for yours, too.

Ambassadors of Hope
Elizabeth Erlandson

On the worst day of my life, I received the same heaven-sent message of comfort from three different people.

Friday, October 13, 2017, was the perfect fall day in Lincoln, Nebraska. Cool. Crisp. Bursting with autumn colors. As much as I loved my job as co-owner of Licorice International, a popular candy store in the downtown tourist district, all I could think about was taking a brisk walk around nearby Holmes Park Lake. I decided to skip work for the afternoon. *Maybe my husband will join me at the lake.*

I picked up my cell phone to call him and was surprised he'd been trying to reach me. He had left four voicemail messages telling me he'd had a minor car accident but assured me that it was no big deal. "I'm fine," he said. "Just meet me on the east side of Holmes Lake."

When I arrived at the park, Doug was on the phone with our insurance agent. The damage to both cars was minimal, and since his car was drivable, we agreed to meet at the body shop and return home in my car.

I pulled out a few seconds before him and glanced in the rearview mirror to make sure he was right behind me. He was for the first few minutes—and then he wasn't. I kept expecting to see his red van crest the hill and catch up with me, but it didn't.

Perplexed, I pulled onto a side street and called him, but he didn't answer. The drive to the repair shop should have taken just a few minutes. *Where is he? What is taking him so long?*

I turned my car around and retraced my route. Eight blocks later, I was stunned to see at least a dozen cars in the middle of the road and several people standing on the sidewalk, peering down a slope. I knew immediately that all those bystanders were staring down at my husband, and my world suddenly shifted. I think I went into shock. A surreal stillness enveloped me, and I felt like an observer in a tragedy, not one of the main characters.

I parked my car, raced across the street, and ran down the incline. Doug's red van was lying on the passenger side, completely crushed. The driver's side had not been damaged. My husband's body lay stretched out on the brown and cream-colored quilt we kept in the back of the van. A man and a woman took turns administering CPR while waiting for emergency help.

> **For this reason, since the day we heard about you, we have not stopped praying for you.**
>
> —COLOSSIANS 1:9 (NIV)

Another accident? So soon? I was too numb to analyze what had happened as I knelt on the grass, stroked Doug's cheek, and whispered in his ear, "Doug, it's Elizabeth. I'm with you. Can you hear me?" He didn't respond. His eyes were wide open, but he couldn't see me. He was barely alive.

The ambulance arrived and whisked Doug away, and I headed back to my car to follow it to the hospital. That's when I encountered the first heaven-sent messenger, a young teacher on her way to the florist to select her wedding flowers. She had witnessed the accident and stopped to help. After seeing me with my husband, she followed me up the hill. "Are you his wife?" she asked.

I nodded. Tenderly yet firmly with intention, she grasped my hand and said, "I want you to know I'm praying for you and your family." And then she was gone.

While driving to the hospital, I called our children, my dear friend Ardith, and our pastors. Six of us gathered in a private room while we waited to hear from the surgeon. We knew Doug had been in an accident, but we still had no idea what caused him to drive off the road. After what seemed an interminable amount of time, we learned that he had not been hurt in the crash, not even a scratch. He had experienced a dissection, a rupture of the lining of the aortic artery, which caused him to bleed internally, and he had lost consciousness, causing his car to run off the road.

Before they wheeled him into surgery, we stood around the gurney and prayed. Then the surgeon looked at me with compassion and said the same words the young woman had spoken: "I am praying for you and your family." He was the second heaven-sent messenger.

Knowing that Doug's surgeon trusted God and believed in the power of prayer comforted me. No matter what happened, I felt confident that Doug was in good hands.

My children and I settled in the waiting room. We hadn't been there long when the third messenger arrived, the police officer who had written the accident report. He explained who he was and handed me a sheaf of papers. "You'll need this for insurance purposes," he said. "I brought it to you personally because I want you to know I'm praying for you and your family."

Doug survived not only the accident and the first open-heart surgery to repair the tear but also a second surgery when his lung cavity filled with fluid three weeks later. Through subsequent procedures too numerous to recount, months of rehabilitation, several falls that required daily wound care, and surgery to repair a popliteal aneurysm, my husband has maintained his optimism and determination to live well. His trust in God has strengthened my faith.

None of this has been easy. Doug no longer drives, and he struggles with balance and memory issues; I am his full-time caregiver. However, whenever I am tempted to feel sorry for myself and question why all this has happened to us, I remember those heaven-sent messengers. I am so thankful that God's people, who believe in the power of prayer, told me they were praying for us that day. The Lord knew I needed assurance of His presence. I believe that's why He sent three ambassadors of hope with the same message: a reminder that I am not alone. No matter what happens, our faithful God is always with me.

> **And the prayer offered in faith will make the sick person well; the Lord will raise them up.**
>
> —JAMES 5:15 (NIV)

Can't Claim Coincidence
Laura Bailey

I am grateful that my husband and I don't often argue, and when we do disagree, the arguments are resolved swiftly. However, not too long ago, we found ourselves in a pretty heated discussion that quickly morphed into a full-on marital spat. There was something I felt we needed to purchase for the home, and my husband couldn't justify the spending; no matter how hard we tried, we were at a standstill. While we have often gone to bed still upset, we've made up by the time we've had our first morning cup of coffee.

Not this time.

It was almost a week of coexisting; never had our house been so quiet! During that week of trading icy glares and the silent treatment, the Lord sent two friends to soften my heart and guide me to seek reconciliation with my husband, Tres, sooner rather than later.

Typically, when my husband and I engage in a marital spat, I vent to my gal pals in the hope of feeling vindicated or, at the very least, blowing off some steam. But not this time. I remained tight-lipped, giving no indications of problems in paradise. If I'm honest, I didn't want to tell them because I knew I was in the wrong—but, pridefully and stubbornly, I wasn't ready to hear advice or even encouragement from well-meaning friends.

On the third day of our continued silent war, I received a call from a childhood friend. At the time I was on the way to dance practice with my three girls in the car, so I silenced the call and told myself I would call her back later. We typically got our families together in the summertime, and with the school year finishing soon, I assumed she was calling to make plans. Since we are both busy with work, families, and other responsibilities, we don't talk often, and it usually takes a massive game of phone tag and a few texts before we finally connect. So I was surprised when I saw a voicemail notification pop up a few minutes later.

After getting the girls settled into their classes, I listened to my friend's message outside. "Hey, I am not sure what's happening, but I needed to call you today. Is everything going OK with you and Tres? I felt the Lord leading me to pray for you all, so I did. But, well, I just hope everything is all right, and know either way, I am praying for your marriage. I am here if you need to talk."

> **Do nothing out of selfish ambition or vain conceit. Rather, in humility value others above yourselves, not looking to your own interests but each of you to the interests of the others.**
>
> —PHILIPPIANS 2:3–4 (NIV)

I replayed the message three more times, and each time I was amazed to hear the words that came out of the speaker. I hadn't spoken to my friend in over a year. We were very close, but our conversations were typically hour-long catch-ups, trying to squeeze in a year's worth of information in an afternoon.

We've talked about our marriages before, but since we both were in pretty spiritually grounded unions by God's grace, it didn't often come up.

My hand lingered over my friend's number, but I stared at the phone instead of calling her back.

My youngest daughter tapped me on the shoulder, breaking my daze. "Mom, it's time to go." On the ride home, I kept mentally replaying the message, finding it a coincidence that she would send it this week. For a brief moment, I pondered that perhaps the Lord was using my friend to nudge me to speak to my husband, but I didn't allow myself to linger on that thought. Instead, we arrived home, we ate dinner, and I went to bed sans conversing with my spouse.

A few more days passed, and my marriage was still at a standstill when I received a text from a friend at church.

"I am praying for you and Tres today," said the message that popped on the screen.

It wasn't odd for her to text me and share that she was praying for me; we were close and often randomly sent prayer requests and encouragement to each other. But this was the first time she mentioned my husband. I quickly responded with a "thank you." What had prompted her to send that message? I was grateful I would see her at church that night so I could find out.

When I asked her about it, she said she'd had a dream that my husband and I had gotten into a big fight and were considering separating. She said she woke up so upset; she'd never felt so worried about a dream before and immediately started praying for us and our marriage. She felt certain it was just a nightmare, but the Holy Spirit led her to reach out to me and pray on our behalf.

I immediately started crying. I shared with her the events of the last few days; while we'd never considered separating, we most certainly hadn't acted like two people who claim to love the Lord and each other. I confessed to her my unwillingness to be the first one to apologize and my childish, selfish behavior.

I was sorry that the dream gave her such a fright, but I was so grateful that she acted on the prompting of the Holy Spirit to reach out to me. God was trying to get my attention and hold my heart through my two friends!

After my husband and I resolved our conflict that night, both apologizing for losing our tempers, we promised never to let our tempers and stubbornness get that out of control again. I always knew we would eventually work through it, but these women's actions led me to seek forgiveness sooner rather than later. The Lord used them and their willingness to be obedient to His leading to guide me to repentance and reconciliation in my marriage. I am so glad they listened and obeyed!

> **. . . with all humility and gentleness, with patience, bearing with one another in love.**
>
> —EPHESIANS 4:2 (ESV)

God Did That

Tracy Ruckman

A golf-ball-sized lump stared at me from the mirror. I'd done my monthly breast exam just 10 days prior and found nothing, but now, this protrusion couldn't be missed.

For decades, I've avoided all things medical. Within my family, I'm well known for being a medical scaredy-cat. My fear of needles was so great that I couldn't look at them, or even think about them, even when others were the ones being stuck. Once, when my boys were teens, my younger son landed in the ER and needed blood tests. When the nurse left the room to retrieve her cart, I stood at the end of his bed, rubbing his feet, assuring him everything would be OK. Suddenly my older son yelled, "Look! Mom's turning green!" They made me sit, and we all had a good laugh, but I never got over the fear.

This lump changed everything.

The moment I discovered it, I began praying, and from that very moment, God surrounded me with His indescribable peace. Yes, literally indescribable. As I pondered all scenarios, I acknowledged that if this lump turned out to be malignant, cancer was not the hardest thing I'd ever faced, so I needed to trust Him and keep moving forward. This lump was no surprise to Him.

Over the course of this journey, God revealed His presence in so many tangible ways that I never felt alone or afraid.

As the early tests began pointing toward breast cancer, I chose to tell only a few friends and close family about the diagnosis. But I knew I could not walk this journey alone, so I enlisted a team of mighty prayer warriors, and they prayed for us faithfully every step of the way for more than 15 months.

My husband has a learning disability and depends on me for most everything, except grooming, bathing, and dressing. He frequently tells people, "She's my secretary, my cook, my chauffeur, and my best friend."

When the lump appeared, I wondered who would take care of him if I got too sick.

That thought sent me into prep mode. When my dad battled cancer, the smell of food cooking made him violently ill, so I hoped to avoid that by cooking as much as my freezer would hold before I started treatments. I cooked and prepared meals and meats to avoid the odors and to make it easy for Tim to eat when I wasn't feeling well.

> **But you, LORD, are a shield around me, my glory, the One who lifts my head high.**
>
> —PSALM 3:3 (NIV)

Since our move in 2020, we've used the laundry facilities in our building or taken clothes to the laundromat, but when I received the cancer diagnosis, friends gifted us with a used set so I could do laundry at home. Their generosity, thoughtfulness, and love were gifts from God.

Prior to my diagnosis, the husband of one friend had a lengthy war with cancer, and the chemo caused him to have bad mouth sores. Snow cones were the only thing that helped him, so when my friend (and prayer warrior) learned of my treatment plan, she sent a shaved ice kit, saying, "I don't want you to suffer like he did." And in fact, it did prevent me from ever getting mouth sores.

Just before my first chemo treatment, another friend also sent a present. She is a cancer survivor whose journey inspired and strengthened me during my own fight. Her beautiful gift of a mug with the word "Courage" handwritten into the clay never fails to remind me of her own faith and courage during her cancer battles. The mug inspired me to continue to press forward.

Between the lumpectomy and the start of chemotherapy, one of my teeth broke. I had hoped what was left would fall out on its own, but instead, the dentist ordered surgery.

My daughter-in-law, Jess, drove me to and from the emergency dental surgery, then announced I was the "least loopy" dental patient she'd ever chauffeured. God used her in another unexpected way to fill a need I didn't know existed. She sat with me through all the lengthy treatment orientations, and through half my chemo treatments (she tore her Achilles' tendon after my third treatment, so she couldn't be there for the others), and she checked on me daily. Her sense of humor and cheerful attitude added a healthy dose of laughter to my recovery.

When chemo started, I learned that I would receive a daily shot for the first seven days after all six treatments. I'm the one with the fear of needles, remember? I also learned that I would have blood tests before each treatment and periodically throughout the entire journey. During my lumpectomy, the surgeon had installed a Medi-port for me to receive the chemo infusions, but the blood work still required individual pokes. Even medical professionals have trouble finding my veins, so I could have feared the whole process. But, with God's healing peace still in my heart, I didn't. I didn't faint or get queasy at any point during any of the sticks or shots, and never felt any of the chemo treatments either, except for one instance the first day, when Jess was with me.

During the middle of the first treatment, I had a sudden odd reaction to one of the chemo drugs. The nurses came running with cool cloths and bottled water, then watched over me for several minutes before going back to their other duties. Toward the end of that treatment, I overhead two of the nurses talking.

"How's Ruckman?"

The nurse and I made eye contact just as Jess said something funny. As I laughed, she said, "Looks like she's doing fine, they're in there laughing!"

God put many other special people on my journey, too. The very day I had the lump examined for the first time, a nurse named Felicia began her new job as oncology navigator in the hospital where I would be sent the following week. She was assigned to my case and walked the entire journey at my side. She helped me process the onslaught of information tossed my way, called between treatments, took notes during office visits so I could focus on the doctor's words, answered all my questions or

> **The LORD will surely comfort Zion and will look with compassion on all her ruins. . . . Joy and gladness will be found in her, thanksgiving and the sound of singing.**
>
> —ISAIAH 51:3 (NIV)

GOD'S GIFT OF TASTE
— Eryn Lynum —

THERE ARE AROUND 400,000 identified species of land plants worldwide. Of those, an estimated 80,000 to 300,000 are edible. Such a vast variety of edible plants reflects God's generous heart.

Scripture portrays God as lavish and abundant in His love and grace. Ephesians 1:7–8 (NIV) talks about "the riches of God's grace that he lavished on us." 2 Corinthians 9:8 (NIV) says, "And God is able to bless you abundantly." God is not stingy, but instead pours out new morning mercies and grace upon grace. One can try a new flavor or food and reflect on a creative God who is far from bland, who is rich in sustenance and joy.

---

concerns, and brought a smile and positive attitude to what could have been a lonely, scary journey.

I finished chemo in September and radiation in mid-November. At the end of the year, I wrote thank-you notes to all the mighty prayer warriors who stood by me, prayed for me, encouraged me, loved me. I recalled all the events and all the people on my journey throughout the year, and I was overwhelmed with gratitude and the sheer beauty I saw behind me. I surprised myself by writing in the first thank-you note, "This year was truly one of the most beautiful years I've ever experienced."

I'm still amazed and awed that a cancer journey could be described as beautiful.

God did that.

More Than a Mountain Hike

Constance B. Fink

Wyoming's 10,200-foot Mount Washburn had towered above our campsite for days, and our curiosity was piqued. Finally, we decided it was time to try to climb to the top.

The road to the mountain started with a gradual incline that went up and up. After many switchbacks, the paved road brought us to a sign that said, "Stop! No vehicle access for the last 1,400 feet. Hiking trail only." We got out of our air-conditioned car and began the walk to the top.

The summit was just above the tree line. It didn't look very far away. Only 1,400 feet of elevation to go. No big deal. An arrow pointed to a footpath just around the curve.

Before locking the car, we had decided we would not need our backpacks, since the ranger station at the end of the trail was in view, and we could get water and other supplies there. It was a warm summer day, and we were looking forward to the cool air at high altitude. My husband and I set out on the 3-mile trail that led to the top. Just 3 miles. Really, no big deal.

We quickly realized we were wrong. The climb was not always gradual—some stretches were quite steep. The ranger station was not always in view, and during the times when the switchbacks took us away from it, it felt as if we were going in the wrong direction.

The tree-lined shaded path quickly turned into a sun-scorched, barren trail. Our pace slowed. My enthusiasm waned. I went from enjoying the lovely mountain path to just wanting to reach the ranger station. But I remembered the words of Hebrews 12—"run with perseverance the race marked out for us"—and pushed myself to continue climbing even when I couldn't see the end goal. I felt my legs begin to strengthen even though my muscles ached. It was a "good" ache. The hike was hard work but good exercise. With every step I chanted to myself, "One step at a time. Pace yourself."

The path leveled out for a bit. We were free to look around without having to navigate jagged rocks underfoot.

Have I made any progress? I asked myself. Yes! The clouds were closer. I could look down at the tops of trees. I noticed how quiet it was. I noticed the breeze. I noticed a songbird. My stride relaxed, and I took deeper breaths.

Expecting to be back in the car in less than an hour, we had left our water bottles behind. But two hours had already passed, and we still had more than halfway to go. The afternoon sun was relentless. Trying to wet my lips with a dry tongue heightened my need and exacerbated my discomfort. Relief and help—either going back to the car or on to the ranger station—were two hours in either direction. The realization brought us to the edge of panic.

We did not know whether to turn back to the car or keep climbing to the summit. Our exhaustion grew with each step. Then, above our complaints and indecision, we heard laughter. Laughter? Were we beginning to hallucinate? But it got louder as two women gallantly walked down the mountain toward us. With smiles on their faces and a bounce in their step, they greeted us. Panting, we returned their greeting with less cheer. They noticed we had no water and, without a second thought, they gave us their bottles to keep. God had sent us exactly what we needed—a generous provision despite our poor judgment to leave our resources behind.

Not only did the two fellow sojourners give water, but they sat with us on the side of the path while we drank the water. We rested. They encouraged. "The view is worth it!" "You can do it!" "Keep going!" "Pace yourself!" "The ranger station has not moved!"

Refreshed from the water and their positive words, we were determined once again—determined to reach the top, not the halfway view. Determined to see it for ourselves, not to hear another's description. We got up and resumed our climb.

With the last turn behind us, we finally climbed the steps to the ranger station. Nothing blocked our view for miles in every direction—we had an eagle's perspective. Just a short time ago, the narrow-wooded path below with tall, gnarly trees had limited my view. The blanket of heavy tree leaves had blocked the sun's light. The jagged rocks and twisted path had slowed my pace, tripping me up and making me worry that I would never reach the top. At times the obstacles had seemed insurmountable.

> **Let us run with perseverance the race marked out for us, fixing our eyes on Jesus, the pioneer and perfecter of faith.**
>
> —HEBREWS 12:1–2 (NIV)

Now I felt like I was soaring, as if I had been carried to the top of the mountain on wings. The warm sun illuminated the mountains, valleys, pastures, and meadows in every direction. We were almost 2 miles high! The variety of colors in the landscape was spectacular. Lush, rolling hills. Snow-capped peaks. Deep crevices. Roaring waterfalls. Brilliant rainbows. Meadows carpeted with wildflowers. The path below us was so small now, insignificant next to the beauty of the mountaintop. I imagine this is how I will feel in heaven—the path of life on earth will be so small in comparison to the majesty around me there.

At the ranger station, we rested. I dozed off and woke to distant thunder. Dark clouds loomed on the horizon and lightning split the sky. The wind kicked up its heels. With each passing minute, the summer storm was getting closer.

We had to get back down the mountain or risk being stuck overnight with no food or water. As we took the first descending steps, we prayed that God would hold back the intensity of the storm and protect us until we reached safety.

Instead, rain poured down on us.

Blinded by the intensity of the storm, we were surprised when we saw a jeep coming toward us. The driver, a park ranger, offered to drive us to the bottom of the mountain. My husband and I looked at each other in amazement.

God did not hold the rain, but rather, His provision reached into the middle of the storm. He is in the threatening storms of life. In the dark woods. On the sun-scorched path. On the sunny mountaintop. He is everywhere.

My child, He reminded me, *I have been with you. Faithfully. Through unexpected unemployment. Through infertility. Through the simultaneous loss of both parents. Through years of a weekend marriage due to an out-of-town job. Through the process of dealing with chronic physical pain. Through the healing from emotional scars. Through dealing with an aging body.*

I will continue to be with you. Always. When you think you cannot survive another disappointment, I am with you and in control. When you feel abandoned, I will never leave you. When you feel sad, I am with you giving comfort. When you feel anxious, I am with you, guarding you. When you feel tired, I am with you, giving strength. When you feel thirsty, my presence will refresh you. When you feel lonely, I am with you, listening attentively. When you feel angry, I am with you understanding your fears.

> "You yourselves have seen . . . how I carried you on eagles' wings and brought you to myself."
>
> —EXODUS 19:4 (NIV)

Back down at the base of the mountain, my spirit was refreshed. With Mount Washburn towering above, I picked up a small rock and put it in my pocket as a keepsake of the whispers and promises that God gave me on that mountain. I will always remember that God is with me. Always.

With renewed strength and motivation from Mount Washburn, I continue to this day on the spiritual climb of life to know and trust Him as my Companion.

When we pray for one another, we enter God's workshop, pick up a hammer, and help him accomplish his purposes.

—Max Lucado

CHAPTER 2

Guided to Bless Others

Speak to Her 42
    Allison Lynn Flemming

An Unlikely Peacemaker. 49
    Toni L. Wilbarger

She Has a Name. 58
    Kristen Paris

Obedience in the Small. 63
    Rachel Wojo

Brunch with a Dear Friend. 66
    Lisa Corduan

Perfect Strangers. 71
    Jennifer S. Niemann

The Small Gift That Made a Huge Impact 76
    Joe Fletcher

Speak to Her ...
Allison Lynn Flemming

There are days that are ordinary and days that are extraordinary, and you have no idea which will be which until you get into the thick of it.

Just a few months earlier, my husband and I had sold everything and moved to Nashville. There we were, two Canadians spending our days writing songs, singing at concerts, and pursuing all our music dreams.

To help make ends meet, I worked for Ben Speer, an artist who was featured on the series *Gaither Homecoming*. Ben was a living legend. The Speer Family singing group were gospel music pioneers. A portrait of Ben and his siblings singing at the White House hung on his office wall, and there was a Grammy on the mantle. A scrapbook contained photos of Ben and his brother, Brock, singing backup vocals for a young Elvis Presley!

But Ben's true passion was his "singing school." Every summer, two hundred students of all ages traveled from across the United States and around the world to spend two weeks singing gospel music. From early morning to late at night, the students studied music theory, songwriting, and learned all the intricacies of building their own music ministries.

I'd been a student myself for a few summers, and when I moved south, Ben offered me a job. I couldn't ask for a better place to work.

One of my main responsibilities was managing student relations. In the months leading up to our summer program, I would spend hours answering questions about the school, what we offered, and what students could expect. Many of our students carried heavy burdens of illness, financial need, or grief, so the calls weren't only about meal programs and class sizes. Often, they just needed to talk, to know they were coming to a safe space.

This was how I first came to know Megan.

Megan had written me early that spring with the standard questions about accommodations and travel arrangements. She was a teenager who loved to sing in her church. Her mom, also a member of their worship team, was going to attend with her.

As our emails went back and forth, I started to learn more about Megan and her mom. That winter, Megan's dad was driving home from work when an impaired driver plowed through a red light and slammed into his car. He died alone in the mangled wreckage. Her mom received a call that night with the terrible news.

> **Anxiety weighs down the heart, but a kind word cheers it up.**
>
> —PROVERBS 12:25 (NIV)

Megan and her mom had been left reeling by the shock of it all. It was now just the two of them, struggling to find their way through the world.

I could relate. A few years earlier, I'd lost my boyfriend, a man I'd planned to marry, to suicide. The circumstances were very different, but I knew that soul-tearing shock. I knew what it was like to have unanswered questions. I knew what it was to have to start life again without the person I loved the most. I knew all about the painful struggle to find that new normal.

Megan had learned of my loss through my blog posts, so in our emails, we shared pieces of our stories. I was glad she and her mom were coming to the school. I prayed it could be a place of healing for them.

On registration day, I found them both and greeted them with hugs; I felt like I knew them so well already. I helped get them organized, and sent them to their dorm room. They both looked bright and cheerful, ready for the fun adventure that lay before them.

Over the next few days, I kept an eye out for Megan. She was meeting friends and attending her classes. She looked like she was doing well. I breathed a little prayer of relief.

Until midweek. I saw her leave her morning voice lesson, and I smiled and waved, but she looked distracted. As she rushed out the door, her vocal coach grabbed my arm and pulled me aside.

"Do you know Megan's story?" I nodded and she continued, "She's having a really difficult day. Something isn't sitting right with her. I think she needs someone to testify to her. I think that should be you."

A knot suddenly twisted in my stomach.

You see, "testify" wasn't really in my skill set. I'd never hidden my Christian faith, but I'd never really volunteered it either. I came from a quietly-live-out-your-faith denomination. Love God, love your neighbor, but leave the preaching to the minister.

The idea of testifying was way beyond my comfort zone. Were there certain words I was supposed to say? What if I said the wrong thing? And what if Megan didn't want someone to testify to her? What if I invaded her privacy and made it all worse?

I smiled at the vocal coach, but inside, I started to pray. *God, Megan needs someone today, but it can't be me. Please send her someone who can say the right thing.*

There. That should handle it.

But as I left the building, I saw Megan walking to her next class. Her face looked dark, her shoulders heavy. I felt a knot in my stomach again, but this time it was different. This didn't feel like fear. Instead, this felt like God nudging me, saying, "Here's your chance. Speak to her."

I quickly turned and walked in the other direction.

We had hundreds of staff and students on campus that week. Many of them were full-time ministers or counsellors. Surely, God would send someone else!

> **Bear one another's burdens, and so fulfill the law of Christ.**
>
> —GALATIANS 6:2 (ESV)

But all day, no matter where I went, I found myself crossing paths with Megan. She'd smile weakly at me, obviously not her normal, cheerful self.

I kept lifting the same prayer, "Please God. Send someone to talk to her!"

Each evening, the students were treated to a concert by a different Christian music group. Because we were in Nashville, top artists donated their time and put on amazing performances for us. The students loved it. No one ever missed a moment of these concerts, staying to the end and buying armfuls of CDs and T-shirts.

That night, our guest artists were rocking the stage with their up-tempo songs and rich harmonies. Every member of the staff and student body was clapping, singing, and cheering. The energy was electric!

Finally, the group gathered around the piano for a ballad. The baritone started a gentle melody, singing about the struggles of this world. The chorus hit, and the quartet burst into harmony, belting out their longing for heaven.

And suddenly, I felt that knot in my stomach again.

Megan, I thought. *This song is going to break Megan's heart.*

Instantly, I felt God nudge me once again. *Go find her.*

I looked around the auditorium but didn't spot her. I slipped into the lobby and checked the washrooms, but she wasn't there. I couldn't find her anywhere in the building. Finally, I looked out the front door.

There was Megan, sitting on a rock in the courtyard, weeping.

I walked across the stone path and sat next to her. For a few moments, we were both quiet.

"That song really hit home, didn't it?" I asked.

She nodded her head and wiped her cheeks as fresh tears filled her eyes.

"I know my dad is in heaven," she started, "but honestly, I just wish he was here."

I felt God keeping me still. *Don't say anything. Just listen.*

She told me everything—all her fears for her future, her concern for her mom, her anxiety around driving, the pain she felt in the smallest everyday moments. Mostly, she spoke of her anger—anger at the drunk driver and anger at God.

After a while, Megan exhaled. She was empty, drained of words, but I could tell we weren't done. Something was still nagging her. She met my eyes and took one more deep breath.

"How did you handle your anger at God?" she whispered.

This was it. This was why I was here in this moment. I wasn't a minister or a counsellor, but I knew what it was to be angry at God for a senseless death. I knew what it was to rail at God with vitriol.

And I also knew about God's grace-filled faithfulness to me in that season. I knew about coming to the other side of that anger, and realizing God had been there the whole time, loving me and offering me strength and grace. I knew what it felt like when that same God, who had heard my cries and felt my rage, turned to me and called me "beloved."

So, I testified. I didn't need perfect words. There was no magic phrase. I just shared the story of God loving me in my most unlovable time. I was honest about my struggle to believe, and equally honest about how much God's love had transformed my broken heart.

> **Rejoice with those who rejoice; mourn with those who mourn.**
>
> —ROMANS 12:15 (NIV)

Megan listened as I poured out my story. Finally, we both sat in silence. We could hear cheers coming through the windows of the auditorium. The concert was coming to an end, and the students were calling for an encore.

"Do you want to go in and catch the final song?" I asked her.

Megan smiled and nodded. She looked brighter, stronger. As we walked back into the building, I turned to her. "There are a lot of people here you can talk to, but just so you know, I'm here for you, anytime."

"Thanks," she said, "I think I'll be OK now."

And she was. She wasn't finished grieving, but there was something about that talk that released her. She enjoyed the rest of the school session. She made friends, and even formed a vocal trio with some other teens. I watched as her mom grew more relaxed, finding peace that her daughter's smile had returned.

I learned such a valuable lesson that night. When God calls us to share our faith, He's not looking for a magic phrase or perfect response. Instead, we're called to honesty, to being authentic. To sharing our story of the God who loves us unconditionally, and who will always nudge us to share that love with others.

An Unlikely Peacemaker

Toni L. Wilbarger

What a beautiful day! I loaded my shopping bags into the car and gazed at the bright blue of the early June sky. My friend Jayne would love the birthday gift I'd purchased, but we still hadn't chosen a date for our celebration. I phoned and left a message, not giving much thought to the missed call. But God soon changed my mind.

Over the next two hours, I dialed Jayne a few more times and texted twice. I even called her roommate, Carol. Neither woman responded. Unease filtered through me, but I reasoned it away. Maybe Jayne's battery had died. No, she always kept her phone charged because she used it for business. After a few more failed attempts, my unease morphed into dread.

Something was wrong.

I prayed for my friends' safety and, at the same time, chastised myself for overreacting. Then God spoke to my heart: *Go to them. Now.* Dread turned into panic. What had happened?

When I arrived, both cars sat in the driveway and the front door stood open. I hurried to the porch and pressed the bell. No one approached. I rang again, my ears picking up the sound of the chime. Surely someone had heard it. I pounded on the storm door.

Enough. I pulled on the handle to let myself in, but it wouldn't budge.

"Jayne! Carol!" My imagination leapt to terrible scenarios. Were they dead from food poisoning? Too sick to move? No. I refused to wander any further in that direction. Assuming they were in the backyard, I turned to head around the side of the house. A movement from inside flashed in my peripheral vision.

Jayne walked toward me and opened the door to let me in. Her white shirt and khaki shorts were wrinkled—very unlike her usual put-together self—and her red-rimmed eyes welled with tears.

"What's wrong?" I asked.

She wandered to the sofa. "Everything's all messed up. Carol won't talk to me anymore, and all we do is fight." She shook her head. "I don't think we can get past this."

"Where is she?" I glanced around the tidy room.

"Outside. Been there for hours." Jayne wiped her eyes.

God, what can I do?

Just listen. They both need to be heard.

I took a deep breath and let it out slowly. "Tell me what's going on."

"Everything. She's getting worse. Her fingers don't work. She can't even write a note or sign a check. Then when I ask her a simple question, she tells me to stop harassing her." Jayne hung her head.

"I thought she was improving. You mentioned her bruises have faded."

Six weeks ago, Carol had flown out west to visit her daughter and grandchildren. She joined in a family pickleball game, but the merriment ended when she fell face first onto the cement. She spent several days in the hospital with swelling of her brain. Carol had seemed to be healing well, but now she was struggling with these new symptoms. I asked Jayne if Carol had visited a doctor since she'd been home.

"No. She says everything will be fine." Jayne bolted from the couch and paced. "It's those people! 'Come on, Mom, let's play pickleball.' Can you imagine? She shouldn't be running around like she's in her thirties."

"It's not their fault."

"You don't get it. When she's here, she's happy. But when she visits them, they talk down to her. They criticize her clothes, her hairstyle, even her faith. She comes home a different person and needs two weeks to shake off their influence. I can't take it anymore." She sighed. "Maybe I should move out."

"Whoa, let's not go there." Their friendship had lasted more than 30 years. "Let me talk to her."

"It won't do any good."

> **Finally, brothers and sisters, rejoice! Strive for full restoration, encourage one another, be of one mind, live in peace. And the God of love and peace will be with you.**
>
> —2 CORINTHIANS 13:11 (NIV)

I wandered past the upright piano in the living room and through the kitchen with its mint-green walls and white cabinets. Exiting through the garage, I stepped into the backyard, blinking against the bright sunlight. Carol sat at a glass picnic table situated on a red brick patio. "Hello?" I greeted her cautiously.

"Oh, hey." As Carol tilted her head slightly to look at me, the sun illuminated her blonde hair. "I thought I heard someone drive up. Sorry I didn't greet you."

"That's OK. Mind if I sit?"

Carol motioned toward one of the remaining chairs. "I suppose she told you what an awful person I am."

God, help me hear with my heart. "She didn't say that."

"She's lost patience with me." Carol reached for a glass that held the remnants of lemonade and melting ice. She left it on the table.

"Maybe a little."

"I wish she'd leave me alone."

I chuckled. "You've known her longer than I have, and we both know that's not happening."

"It's not funny anymore."

Heat flashed onto my face. "No, of course not. Just trying to lighten the mood."

"Yeah, well, that's not happening either."

God, I'm tanking here. Guide me. I tried again. "How are you feeling?"

Carol turned toward me. A faint, greenish-yellow tinge covered her nose and surrounded her eyes where the bruises had faded. "I'm better. Really."

"Jayne mentioned you're having trouble with your hands."

"It comes and goes. I'll be fine." She waved me off.

"Jayne's worried about you and, frankly, so am I. Maybe you should see a doctor."

"Please stop. I'm tired of being treated like a child."

God, this isn't going well.

We sat in silence for a few moments, and the scent of a neighbor's barbecue filled the air. Carol continued. "Jayne blames my family, but she doesn't understand. Yes, their opinions are different from mine, but I respect their beliefs. But she acts like they have some kind of hold over me."

"Jayne says they make you feel bad about yourself."

"I know what she thinks." Carol shifted away.

Why did I repeat Jayne's argument? Shouldn't I have said something to bring peace? Instead, I'd poured more fuel on the fire. "I'm sorry. I didn't mean to muddy things."

Carol fixed her pale blue eyes on me. "They're my *children*. What am I supposed to do, disown them?" She leaned her head back and closed her eyes. "I'm so tired. I'm sure that's what's wrong. I just need more sleep."

I tried to think of something constructive to add. I understood both sides of the conflict, but I didn't know how to bridge the gap between my friends. I wiped perspiration from my forehead. "Let me talk to Jayne again." I patted Carol's shoulder as I left.

"Well?" Jayne looked up from the couch.

I settled next to her. "You're right about Carol ignoring her symptoms." I breathed deeply, steeling myself for what I had to say next. "But blaming her family doesn't help."

"It's the truth."

> **Then I heard the voice of the Lord saying, "Whom shall I send? And who will go for us?" And I said, "Here am I. Send me!"**
>
> —ISAIAH 6:8 (NIV)

"Try to see it from her point of view. Her family lives several states away. When she spends time with them, she wants everything to be easy. She refuses to ruffle feathers. If that means putting her own opinions aside, then so be it."

"She doesn't just keep her thoughts to herself. She changes her entire personality."

"Maybe. But that's her choice."

Jayne ran her fingers through her curly, light brown hair and slumped into the sofa cushions. "It's a bad one."

"You can't fix her. You know that, right?"

"I suppose."

The air conditioner switched on, its hum breaking into the silence. I wondered what more I could say. *OK, God, now what? Bring them together.*

"You two should talk." I made my way back to Carol and asked her to join Jayne in the living room.

"No." She shooed a bumblebee from the edge of her empty glass.

"Look, you've been out here for hours and all you have to show for it is a sunburn. If it helps, I'll sit with you both." Birds chattered in the trees while I waited for her response.

Finally, Carol sighed and followed me. She didn't acknowledge Jayne as she took the chair on the opposite side of the room. I sat between them and sent up a quick prayer: *Help me get through to them.*

When neither woman spoke, I started the conversation. "OK, here goes. Carol, I agree with Jayne that you need to go back to the doctor. Your symptoms are preventing you from accomplishing even ordinary tasks."

"See?" Jayne said.

"Why don't you just—" Carol started.

"Hold it!" My voice sounded harsh, and I winced. *I'm not good at this, God. Help!* "Forgive me for yelling. Let's start over. Carol, Jayne thinks you wouldn't have played pickleball in the first place if you hadn't been trying to please your family. She knows how to stand up for herself, and she wishes you could too. Her frustration is what causes her to lash out.

"And Jayne, you've always known Carol's personality is different than yours. You can't change her." I lowered my voice. "Only God can."

Jayne wiped her eyes and Carol twisted her hands in her lap. But they still refused to speak. I continued, "OK, perhaps we can reach a compromise. Jayne?"

She barely glanced my way.

"If Carol agrees to see the doctor, will you drop the complaints against her family?"

Jayne cleared her throat. "I'll try."

"What about it, Carol? Will you make an appointment?"

Carol looked at me, then down at her fingers. "I guess so."

"Good. Now, do I need to call you in a couple days to check on you?"

> **In their hearts humans plan their course, but the LORD establishes their steps.**
>
> —PROVERBS 16:9 (NIV)

They both declined, but they still averted their gazes. I bit my lip. "I can't stand this. Will you please look each other in the eye?"

They started to turn toward each other but didn't complete the gesture.

"No, this won't do," I said. "Get up, both of you." From their expressions, I decided they thought I was crazy. But they stood.

"Now give each other a hug," I commanded.

Jayne rolled her eyes.

"Go on." But neither moved. "Here, you stick out your arms like this." I demonstrated and observed a slight smile on Carol's face. They engaged in what could only be called the briefest of embraces before they backed away.

GOD'S GIFT OF TOUCH
— Kimberly Shumate —

WHEN THE FIRST frost touches the plants and trees, it must bring a shudder to them. When water touches the rocks in a riverbed, it is at home as its current sweeps over them. When the kiss of a loved one brushes our cheek, a swell of tenderness consumes us. When we are struck on the cheek, we feel the impact of injury and rejection. Just one touch can make or break our sense of value. Yet God's touch is the only touch that can bring complete restoration. His soothing caress brings peace on contact and healing in His fingertips.

"Nope," I said. "Do it again, this time like you mean it."

Finally, they grasped each other tightly, and I noticed fresh tears in Jayne's eyes. "I'm sorry."

"Me too," Carol said.

Thank You, God. I spoke with them for another 30 minutes to reassure myself they would be OK. Then I gathered my purse, slipped into my sandals, and started for the door. They both hugged me.

"I don't know what we would have done if you hadn't stopped by," Jayne said. "Why did you, anyway?"

When I explained how God led me, their eyes widened. Jayne nodded. "I prayed for a resolution. I never would have guessed He'd send you."

I chuckled. "To tell you the truth, I'm as shocked as you are."

As I drove home, I thanked God for using me to help my friends and for guiding me through the last few hours.

Carol and Jayne reconciled after that, and remain fast friends to this day. Carol did go to the doctor, and in follow-up testing they discovered a brain bleed—one with potentially harmful long-term effects, but now, by God's grace, she's made a full recovery. And to this day, every time I remember what happened I marvel at how perfectly God orchestrated events. I'd started the day purchasing things that wouldn't last, but I'd concluded it by securing a treasure far more valuable than anything in my shopping bags.

She Has a Name

Kristen Paris

Perhaps I shouldn't have browsed through that catalog. My propensity to buy things I didn't need had been a way of coping with stress, frustration, and even fear. I'd gotten better over time. It had been quite a while since I'd made an unnecessary purchase, and I wanted to keep that streak going to prove to myself that I wasn't materialistic or frivolous. Besides, we really couldn't afford extras.

But browse I did, and something caught my eye. At least it wasn't for myself this time, or even for our children, who really didn't need anything new.

It was springtime, and a pink tulip design on a two-page spread of merchandise practically sang out the joy of the season of life renewed. The personalized stationery set called out to my inner shopper. A close friend of mine loved pink tulips. This pattern was particularly appealing because it was bordered by a soft spring green, a favorite color of hers. It couldn't have been more well suited to my friend if she had designed it herself.

I hesitated. It wasn't her birthday; that had recently passed. It wouldn't be appropriate for Christmas. But it was perfect for her, and I smiled as I thought of her eyes lighting up in delight. I knew I had to buy it.

My frugal streak withered. I chose a feminine font to personalize it with her name, Debbie, and ordered. These were the days before next-day delivery, so I had to wait several weeks. Patience isn't my strong suit, and I think I was more anxious over this simple gift than I'd ever been for anything I'd ordered for myself. This purchase just felt right, and I hoped it was as pretty in person as it was in the catalog.

The box finally came, and I ripped it open excitedly. The stationary was gorgeous, exceeding my expectations, and I couldn't wait to give it. I knew I should save it for Christmas. But it was May. Christmas was a long time away.

I debated. Now that I had it in my hand, my impulse purchase seemed a bit silly. I knew she'd love it, but there wasn't an occasion to celebrate, or a natural opportunity to give it to her. Why had I caved to an impulse when I'd been so good lately about not spending money? Guiltily, I took it to the "gift closet" where I hid Christmas gifts from our kids, but then I couldn't bring myself to hide it away there. After all, the purchase had been made, and I couldn't send it back, because it was personalized. Mostly, though, I just ached to give it to her. Now.

> **The LORD is close to the brokenhearted and saves those who are crushed in spirit.**
>
> —PSALM 34:18 (NIV)

I hadn't heard from my friend for a little while, which was unusual. We used to get together often for coffee, tea, or walks through the pine forest near my home. But lately, she had been a bit more distant. Uncertain whether I should bother her, I stood indecisively for several minutes. Finally, I wrapped the set in a pretty gift bag with pink tissue paper, headed to her house, and left it on the doorstep. I was pretty sure she'd know who it was from.

I was correct.

A few days later, we walked together again, meandering down our favorite trail as we hadn't done for a while. The pensive mood she'd been in lately seemed lifted a bit, and she opened up about the downward spiral her thoughts had been taking recently. With tears in her eyes, she told me what my small gift had meant to her.

The day I brought it over, she had hit her lowest point. The feeling had been looming for some time, growing in the deep recesses of her heart where no human eye sees. Like many a homeschool mom at the end of her teaching tenure, she'd been feeling useless and unnecessary. Her kids were nearly grown, and technically didn't need her to get through the motions of daily life anymore. As a stellar homemaker, her life revolved around family. Those of us who serve our loved ones day in and day out as our primary occupation are particularly affected by normal life changes like children growing up and depending on us less. Without performance reviews, raises, or office meetings where we can be seen, it's easy to feel insignificant, even worthless. This can lead to questioning of one's value and purpose in living.

"My husband would be fine without me. My kids are self-sufficient. They don't need me. They'd be fine too," she told me.

"I had a plan," she whispered hesitantly, tears welling in her eyes. That got my attention, and she was no longer the only one with tears in her eyes. I wondered how I had missed seeing her grief and desperation. She didn't expand on her "plan," and I didn't ask, as it felt too personal. I understood. Life had no longer seemed worth continuing. I'd been in that dark place too at times. I knew that empty feeling all too well.

Her tone grew more hopeful. "When I saw your gift, it reminded me—I have a name."

She repeated the statement as tears spilled over for both of us. "I have a name."

In a stronger tone, with a tentative but heartfelt smile, she continued, "I am known. I am significant. I mean something to someone. I'm not nobody. I have a name."

To this day, I don't know exactly how deep her depression went in that season. These things are hard to fully understand when we're not the one going through them, no matter how deeply we love those who are. But God knows. He saw her. He heard her heart's cry. And He answered through a simple set of stationery, emblazoned with her name.

I wondered what might have happened had I not fallen prey to my shopping habit. What if I had been strong, resisting the urge to purchase something totally unnecessary by any practical standard? I've since learned to throw catalogs away without looking at them, though online shopping makes overspending a constant temptation. But I'm grateful for that one slipup, when God used my weakness for good.

> **For it is God who works in you to will and to act in order to fulfill his good purpose.**
>
> —PHILIPPIANS 2:13 (NIV)

He saw her need, and knew what would speak to her when that need grew deepest. He'd heard my prayers that I be a tool in His hand and knew exactly how to best use me. He even knew the precise timing that would bring together each detail perfectly, from the day the catalog arrived in the mail to the moment she found the gift on her doorstep.

Years have passed, and our friendship has deepened as we have walked through life together. We've celebrated, mourned, laughed, and yelled in frustration, trusting and caring for each other's hearts. Debbie has helped me far more than I ever could help her, particularly when I've struggled through dark days of my own. I can't count the number of times she has "coincidentally" called at just the right instant to keep me from doing something foolish, or when I needed a listening ear. It may be our friendship, but it's also God's tool for shaping us, comforting us, encouraging us, and sometimes confronting us.

> "I have summoned you by name; you are mine."
>
> —ISAIAH 43:1 (NIV)

I couldn't have known the unspoken need of my friend's heart, but God did. To me, it was an impulse purchase. From God, it was both a lifeline and a love note.

I ordered a mere gift, but God had ordered my steps.

She has a name: a name God knows. So do you.

Obedience in the Small
Rachel Wojo

As a mother of five, I'm no stranger to the daily chaos of life. Between the kids' activities, household chores, and keeping up with work, time is a precious commodity.

Yet, on one particularly hectic day, I felt an unmistakable tug on my heart as I drove out of my neighborhood subdivision. God was impressing upon me to take a greeting card and a gift card to a neighbor's home. The first time I drove past the house, I felt the Holy Spirit whisper, *They need your help.* It wasn't audible, but I knew it was from God because I wouldn't have thought of it on my own.

It seemed like such a small thing; honestly, I wasn't even sure why I felt this nudge. But I knew enough to listen when God spoke to my heart, even when His promptings didn't make logical sense at the time.

At first, I hesitated. I immediately began to rationalize: *Do I really have time for this today? What if it's awkward? What difference can a simple greeting card and gift card make?* But the prompting wouldn't leave me. Toward evening, after driving past this home several times as I chauffeured children to sports activities, I told my husband what I knew I needed to do.

"You might think I'm crazy," I said to him, "but I need to stop at the grocery store to grab a greeting card and gift card."

"For what?" he asked. I explained briefly, and he smiled. "Whatever you need to do, honey."

He dropped me off at the grocery store door, and I ran in. I grabbed a card, scribbled a few encouraging words, and enclosed a gift card that could be used at the grocery store, wondering if this small gesture would even matter. It felt strange to leave the envelope blank; however, I had no idea to whom it should be addressed. Yet I couldn't shake the feeling that I was supposed to do this.

> **But the Advocate, the Holy Spirit, whom the Father will send in my name, will teach you all things and will remind you of everything I have said to you.**
>
> —JOHN 14:26 (NIV)

As I approached my neighbor's house, something about the short walk felt weighty. I knocked on the door, feeling a strange combination of anticipation and uncertainty. When the door opened, a woman stood there.

"Hi. This may seem a little strange, but I feel like I am supposed to drop this off here today." I smiled and handed her the greeting card, hoping she wouldn't think I was completely crazy.

"I'm not the homeowner, but I'll give this to her," she said.

Then another woman appeared, the open greeting card still in her hand; I noticed the tears welling up in the corners of her eyes.

"I don't know how you knew to come," she said, her voice breaking. "But thank you."

What she shared next caught me off guard. The day before, her friend's daughter had taken her own life. My neighbor's home had become the gathering place for those grieving this tragic loss. The weight of her sorrow was palpable, and as I stood there, I realized the magnitude of what was happening.

"I've been wondering how we're going to feed everyone who's here," she said, wiping away her tears. "I didn't know what we were going to do. And then you showed up."

I was speechless. At that moment, I realized this wasn't just about a gift card for groceries. This was about God's perfect timing. What seemed like a small, perhaps even insignificant gesture was a tangible answer to a need she hadn't yet voiced to anyone. God had known all along. He had orchestrated the moment down to the second.

It was as if the atmosphere in that doorway shifted. The grief was still there, but there was now something else—hope.

As I walked away from that home, I couldn't stop thinking about how easily I could have missed that moment. If I had allowed my schedule, doubts, or desire for comfort to rule my actions, I would have missed the opportunity to be a small part of God's provision for that family. Too often I've brushed aside those small promptings, not realizing the potential impact, and I wonder how many of those chances I've missed in the past. But this time, I didn't miss it. And because of that, I got to witness something beautiful—God's love and provision at the exact moment it was needed.

Sometimes God's presence looks like a gift card. Sometimes it looks like showing up at just the right moment. And sometimes, our simple acts of obedience reveal His perfect timing amid our ordinary days.

Brunch with a Dear Friend

Lisa Corduan

Saturday mornings were reserved for my husband, Ralph, and me—just the two of us. A time to reconnect with quiet conversation and a Bible study. We were very much creatures of habit, and our usual spot for brunch was a corner booth at a local bakery. But one autumn Saturday, things became anything but routine as I received a prompt from God.

Ralph and I were on the interstate on our way to our usual spot when I found myself making an unusual suggestion.

"Should we try that little deli on Sunset Boulevard this morning?" As the words left my mouth, I thought, *Where did that come from?*

"But we always go to Harbison." Ralph replied. "We know what we like there. Besides, Sunset's in the other direction."

"OK. It was just a thought." I smiled and turned to the window.

Without further discussion, however, Ralph set the blinker and maneuvered the car into the right lane. We took the next exit, turned around and headed toward Sunset Boulevard.

After we placed our order at the deli counter, we slid into a corner booth. Our Bibles and notebooks were spread across the table; we bowed our heads to pray. But the environment in this restaurant was very different. Noisy. Crowded. Distracting.

A group of ladies at the neighboring table were in a heated discussion. Their voices carried angry, bitter words as they plotted how one could secure "permanent" alimony from a soon-to-be former spouse. The volume and tone of their conversation hindered our attempts to talk.

"Can we change tables?" I packed up our Bibles and books. Thankfully our food had not yet come, which made moving easy.

The only other table available stood right in the middle of the floor among many other distractions—clanking coffee cups and chit-chat as patrons filled their cups at the coffee kiosk that stood near us. Music blared from the speaker above our table. A woman sitting behind us engaged in a series of phone calls at a volume that rivaled both our previous divorce-discussing neighbors and our overhead concert.

"I'm sorry I suggested we come here. I don't know what I was thinking." I tried to focus on the Bible study.

"You want to just go home? We can do the study next week." Ralph lifted his cup to his lips. "I would like more coffee before we leave."

"The noise doesn't bother you?"

Ralph shook his head.

"If you want to keep going, I'll try not to let everything distract me so much."

"You sure?"

> **What other nation is so great as to have their gods near them the way the LORD our God is near us whenever we pray to him?**
>
> —DEUTERONOMY 4:7 (NIV)

I nodded.

"OK, if you're sure." Ralph returned to the question in our study guide. "So, what does 'grace' mean to me?" As he elaborated on his response, an overpowering urge to pray with and for him stirred in my soul.

"I would like to pray." I reached across the table and closed my hands around his.

"What are you doing?" He glanced around the room, then searched my face.

He knew this was unusual behavior for me. I love prayer and being in the presence of God. Sharing a quiet, intimate moment with my Lord. I am not ashamed of praying in public—closing my eyes, bowing my head, acknowledging the conversation with God. But it was difficult for me to speak a prayer out loud in public. Yet, sitting in the middle of the restaurant—not tucked away in our usual corner—I prayed. Out loud.

We opened our eyes. I released Ralph's hands and relaxed back into my chair until I caught a glimpse of the woman at the table behind us. Her phone, now silent, was clutched in her left hand. She sat at the very edge of her seat. The fingers on her right hand tapped against the tabletop as she leaned forward. It was as if she were waiting to be released from her chair. She was watching us intently. I searched my memory. Did I know her? Why was she staring? Did she want to talk to us? To me? Our eyes met three or four times. I nodded. She did not respond.

Moments later, Ralph and I were deep in discussion over a particular verse. Our attempts to interpret the context seemed to be in vain, despite consulting numerous commentaries on his phone. So we did what we often do in this situation—Ralph called his brother, a retired theology professor and our favorite resource for all things related to theology. While Ralph was on the phone, I again felt an overwhelming urge deep in my soul. This time it was accompanied by a thought: *Get more water.* A glance at my glass, more than half full, made me chuckle, and I thought, *I don't need more water.* Yet I rose from my seat, guzzled the glass of water—it would be foolish to fill an already full glass—and made my way to the drink station.

As I placed the cup on the counter to secure the lid, I saw the woman from the nearby table, the one I had noticed before, had positioned herself at the coffee kiosk. She now stood between me and my table, and she kept glancing at me. I considered walking around, but instead began walking toward her, shifting to the left side of the aisle to allow her plenty of room.

She stepped backward, away from the counter, and stood in the middle of the aisle.

I stepped farther to my left to move around her.

She turned to face me and extended her hand to touch my arm. "I was so blessed to see you two pray together. It's such a sweet thing that you can pray with each other."

> **"And surely I am with you always, to the very end of the age."**
>
> —MATTHEW 28:20 (NIV)

"Oh, thank you. That's kind of you to say."

"My name is Pam." She told me she was a Christian, but she had lost her way for more than a year and was trying to come back to God. I invited her to come back to our table and sit with us.

At the table, I introduced Pam to Ralph. She explained she was living with her boyfriend in a hotel room but was trying to leave the relationship. She had no job and very little money. To make things worse, someone had just stolen a part off her truck, leaving her stranded. During the next several moments, we shared about God's faithfulness and grace. His desire to bring us all home to Himself. We recounted stories of prodigal sons and our own wayward behaviors.

I thought about how God had seemed far from us recently, too. Like most people, our schedules were overcrowded: jobs, kids, household projects, homework, sports activities. The list went on and on. Life was hectic. Time was short. Weeks turned into months without seeing friends, and I was especially missing the time with our dearest friend of all—God. Where was His promise to always be near?

Now, as we talked with Pam about God's promise, it was a reminder to myself, too. *God is always near us.* I believe He called us to this deli to minister to Pam, but at the same time, He was ministering to us, too.

Neither Ralph nor I carry much cash, but what little we had we gave to her just as the tow truck arrived. She thanked us, saying, "Oh, bless you. I didn't know how I would pay for the tow." Before our good-byes, we all bowed our heads and Ralph prayed for Pam.

After she left, Ralph and I returned to our Bible study. The distractions were still the same, and yet I didn't seem to notice anymore.

There we sat, like any other Saturday. Just the two of us— and the Holy Spirit. My Heavenly Father and dear friend God was with me. Just like He promised.

Perfect Strangers
Jennifer S. Niemann

The dollar store teemed with shoppers this morning. I made a beeline to the card aisle, focused on accomplishing a long list of errands. Then, overhearing a woman's voice from the other side of the card rack, I stopped, not wanting to intrude.

"He won't even talk to us. I'm buying him a birthday card to let him know we still care, but I doubt we'll hear back from him."

Peeking around the rack, I spied a woman speaking on her cell phone. What to do? I always felt uncomfortable shopping next to people having private conversations on their phones.

Pulling out my errand list, I counted six separate stops, each at a different store. I checked the time—only two hours before an appointment at home. If I didn't hurry, I wouldn't finish them all. Fidgeting, I waited to hear the woman say goodbye, then continued into the aisle.

As I picked up a card to read, the woman said, "It's so hard finding the right birthday card for Matthew. He has autism, so I don't want anything too mushy."

"I can understand that," I mumbled, mindful of my time. Glancing sideways, I noticed she was petite with long gray hair covering the side of her face.

She showed me the card in her hand. "This one might work for him. It seems pretty simple," she continued. "You see, his mom hasn't been in his life for a long time, so I've tried to be available to him. But lately, he just quit talking to us." She went on to explain that she was a widow, living with her son. Matthew was a young relative she had helped raise.

"I'm sorry to hear that," I replied.

Feeling a nudge in my spirit, I recognized that this woman could use a listening ear. After 30 years of walking through life with God, I recognized this feeling. Quietly, He reminded me that my agenda needed to be flexible enough to fit into His. It was time to pay attention to where God might be at work.

I turned to engage her. "Why won't Matthew talk to you, do you know?"

"I'm not sure. He refuses to go to church with us anymore. He's isolating in his apartment, playing computer games all day and not going to work." The woman paused, looking down at the floor. "His friends aren't the best influences, and he's questioning his identity."

"Oh, my," I responded, choosing my words carefully. "I see why you're concerned. I have friends and family members with some of these same issues and have dealt with them in nursing as well. I think it's great that you're still reaching out to him in love."

"I bet he might do better if he moved closer, but I can't convince him if he won't talk or answer the phone," she continued.

"That's hard," I agreed. The young man's situation sounded worrisome. Being gifted with an empathetic heart, I continued asking questions. The woman shared Matthew's struggles with mental illness on top of autism. I mentioned some community resources in our county that came to mind.

"What church do you guys attend?" I asked. She told me that she and her family were trying a new church in the area, which they seemed to enjoy. Since she liked Bible study,

I mentioned the one I helped facilitate at my church. We sure had a lot in common!

Near the end of our conversation, I decided to forge ahead. "By the way, what is your name? May I pray for you and your family?"

"My name is Bonnie," she answered, tears blurring her eyes. "Would you really do that?"

"Absolutely, Bonnie! I would be honored to pray for all of you. I can even give you my name and number to text prayer requests, or we can talk again if you'd like."

"Well, that would be great!" Bonnie responded. "I've worried so much about Matthew lately—but I know that prayer works!"

"It certainly does!" I heartily agreed. "Which is why we need to ask God for His help!"

Bonnie and I exchanged phone numbers and set up a time to call for prayer. Before I left, God brought one more thing to mind.

> "My command is this: Love each other as I have loved you."
>
> —JOHN 15:12 (NIV)

"Hey, Bonnie. Can you use this, maybe in Matthew's birthday card?" I pulled out a five-dollar fast-food gift card from my wallet. "I almost forgot about it. One of my friends sent this at Christmas with instructions that I should look for someone to bless with it."

"Oh, yeah! I can do that," she said, taking the card from me. "And if he doesn't want it, I could use it, if that's OK?"

"Certainly!" I nodded.

"You've been a godsend!" Bonnie announced. "Did you know this was my first time in this dollar store? I usually go to a different one. I think the Lord sent you along at just the right time."

I smiled, my heart glad. Errands could wait. "Yes, He did, Bonnie. He's good like that!"

Leaving the store, I admonished myself over my reluctance to surrender time from my packed schedule. If I was honest, my first reaction on such a busy day was to avoid other shoppers instead of engaging in conversation.

Hopping in my car, I headed over to the next store. I needed to save two errands for another day, but that no longer bothered me. Instead, I felt comforted knowing I was in the right place at the right time.

God's plan superseded my own that morning. Our meeting certainly felt orchestrated—the fact that we were both praying sisters in Christ along with my experiences with mental health and autism seemed beyond coincidence. God must've known we'd be a good match when he landed us in the same aisle!

Over the following months, Bonnie and I nurtured our new friendship through texts and weekly prayer calls. One morning, I awoke to a text from Bonnie asking me to call her, as she had some news.

"Guess what happened this past weekend!" she reported. "Matthew reached out and came to visit, then stayed overnight with us!"

> **Let us not become weary in doing good, for at the proper time we will reap a harvest if we do not give up.**
>
> —GALATIANS 6:9 (NIV)

"Wow, Bonnie, that's great! An answer to our prayers for sure!"

Imagine if I had buzzed off too quickly from the dollar store that morning. I would have missed the blessings of a new friendship and the sweet joy of answered prayer. We never know whom God might bring across our path next.

The Small Gift That Made a Huge Impact
Joe Fletcher

I had never taken a mission trip outside of the US, and I was eager for an adventure. I ran into Peter, an American evangelist who had spoken at our church. He was looking for an opportunity to expand his ministry beyond our nation's borders. Sam was a friend and a member of our church. He was from India, and had a heart to share the gospel in his native country. The three of us began talking about short-term ministry opportunities in India. Before long, we were on an Air India plane headed to New Delhi. We would be gone for almost a month.

The day after we arrived in India, Peter spoke at a Baptist church in Jaipur. From there we traveled to a Christian school where almost all of the students' parents were Hindu. These parents did not enroll their children in this school because it was Christian. Rather, they put their children in that school because it was known to offer an excellent education—they only tolerated the Christianity part. There, I had the honor of speaking and sharing the Gospel at a special program for the parents. It was a tough crowd, but in general, I was received politely.

By far the most memorable part of our trip was ministering in the tribal areas in the state of Gujarat. Each evening we would hold very large meetings where we would preach about

Jesus. Thousands would come to these meetings. Many would walk several kilometers to get there.

The tribal people lived extremely humble lives. The area was beautiful and peaceful, lush and green with water buffalo roaming freely through the fields, but the poverty of the area was on a different level than anything I'd seen before. Most of the tribal people that we served lived in thatch-roofed homes and worked in the rice paddies all day, earning just enough so that their families would not starve.

Several times we were invited to share a meal in someone's home, and we felt it would be rude to reject the invitation. The people went to great lengths to feed us. We knew that in some cases when they served us chicken, it meant that their family would not eat meat again for a month. It was humbling. But it was also hazardous. Whenever we ate with one of the tribal families, it was inevitable that either Peter or I would get sick. Oddly, we rarely got sick at the same time, and Sam and other native Indians who were traveling with us never seemed to suffer any ill effects. They explained Peter's and my seemingly random reactions away by saying that Americans had "weak" systems. I began to dread any kind of local hospitality!

> **Jesus then took the loaves, and when he had given thanks, he distributed them to those who were seated. So also the fish, as much as they wanted.**
>
> —JOHN 6:11 (ESV)

Toward the end of our trip, we were invited to eat in the home of a very poor family. On this occasion Peter had stayed

GOD'S GIFT OF TASTE
— Eryn Lynum —

GOD FASHIONED INGREDIENTS with five familiar flavors: sweet, sour, bitter, salty, and savory. One type of savory flavor is referred to as umami, a difficult-to-describe taste that is found in hearty broths, meat, fermented foods, and mushrooms. Umami is a much-sought-after flavor in different types of cuisine because it is known to be deeply satisfying, the essence of full flavor.

In Ephesians 3:19, the apostle Paul prays that the believers will know the love of Christ "that surpasses knowledge—that you may be filled to the measure of all the fullness of God" (NIV). Enjoying an expertly crafted meal can call to mind the One who crafted every flavor, and ultimately satisfies every desire and need with His fullness of love.

---

back at our hotel. It was his turn to be sick. This family was so poor that, even if they sacrificed, they could not afford to feed us chicken. Nevertheless, it was important to them for us to eat in their home. They apologized over and over that they could not serve us a fancy meal.

There were fruit trees growing near their home. As we were sitting at the table, our host brought out a very large bowl of peeled mango and papaya. That was it. That was the meal. Although the family clearly felt awkward serving us such a simple meal, I was ecstatic. The fruit was sweet and juicy! There was no chicken to make me ill. There was none of the spicy food that burned my mouth, a staple of Indian cuisine that I was glad to be free of for a night.

The family quickly saw how thrilled I was from the way I gobbled my fruit, and it put them at ease. After I had finished all the fruit that had been served on my plate, our host removed that plate and put the entire serving bowl of fruit in front of me! Everyone laughed. I will never forget how much I enjoyed that meal. Neither will I forget the joy that this family had as they saw how much their generosity was appreciated.

When resources are limited, we sometimes may feel that the little we can give won't accomplish much. But when we truly dedicate ourselves and our gifts to the Lord, He can cause even a small gift to make a huge impact—to bring joy we might never have expected. Whenever I have the ability to give only a little, I remember the example of the loaves and fishes the little boy gave to Jesus. And I fondly remember my glorious meal of mango and papaya!

God gives us friends. He uses people to shape our hearts to be more like His, and He uses us to shape others. It's messy along the way, but worth the effort.

—Bob Goff

CHAPTER 3

Blessings of Friends and Family

The Gift. 82
    Jennifer S. Niemann

A Difficult Love 86
    Jeanne Takenaka

A God of Miracles 92
    Susan Shumway

When the Strong Hit the Wall 98
    Lynne Hartke

Meeting God in Mama's Garden 104
    Cheryl Wyse

Grandpa's Priceless Gifts 109
    Krystal Boelk

The Gift

Jennifer S. Niemann

Shivering, I wrapped my fuzzy blue robe tighter around my body. The view from my second-story office window revealed fat snowflakes swirling around furiously in the mid-March darkness. How disheartening! I pulled the curtains together to shut out the return of winter.

Grabbing a throw blanket, I curled into my favorite recliner. The low rumbling of a delivery truck turning onto our dead-end street surprised me. *Isn't it almost 8 p.m.? What a messy night to be out making deliveries!* I thought.

I paid little attention until the truck downshifted and turned, headlights flashing across our upper windows. *Wait, did that delivery truck turn into our driveway? Did I order anything?* My memory came up blank, but I knew my husband often received deliveries for work at our home.

The truck door slammed, heavy boots clomped down the sidewalk, and then a *ding dong* rang out as the deliverer dropped the package and retreated.

I tried yelling from the top of the stairs. "Honey! You've got a package! Can you get that?" But there was no response, only loud music ascending from my husband's basement office.

Sigh. I would have to go down to retrieve it myself.

Wearily I descended the stairs and waited at the side windows until the truck left our driveway. With some effort, I hauled open our frozen front door. Icy wind propelled a burst of determined flurries inside as I stooped to retrieve the package.

Shoving the door closed with my shoulder, I headed toward the basement stairs to bring the package to my husband. As I stepped into the kitchen light, I noticed that the package I had assumed was for him was addressed to me instead.

A package for me? But I didn't order anything! And my birthday was over a week ago.

Confused, I ripped open the protective paper covering and pulled out a rectangular box. Spying gift receipts inside, I snatched them up, hoping to discover a clue to the sender. But they yielded no help. The paper message simply read, "Enjoy your gift," and the sender remained anonymous.

A friend loves at all times, and a brother is born for a time of adversity.

—PROVERBS 17:17 (NIV)

Someone sent me an anonymous gift? That had never happened before.

I sliced open the box and pulled out the foam protection. Nestled inside rested a beautiful Willow Creek figurine of a woman, her shoulders and head aimed heavenward and her arms straight outward, enabling three little bluebirds to perch.

What a beautiful picture of joy and release. It captivated me. The card inside announced the title: "Happiness."

Happiness. Exactly what I needed, but which seemed so far away.

The previous March, I'd almost beaten the chronic health issues I'd been battling for 5 years. I'd felt so much better. But by fall, I found myself in a full-blown relapse. When my illness flared, everyday activities such as eating and sleeping became unpredictable and difficult. None of the usual treatments worked. As winter closed in and the days become shorter and colder, the situation spiraled out of control, and I began to despair. Hopes for healing turned bleak, plunging me into depression.

I didn't want to admit, even to myself, how badly I was struggling. Holding on to a strong faith, I stayed active in my church's women's ministry and a Christian writing group. How would it be seen if I expressed my negative feelings? Would I be judged as weak in faith or unable to cope? On the other hand, could my honesty help others relate?

No stranger to depression, I'd struggled through dark valleys earlier in my life. To my dismay, I found myself in the midst of them again. I weighed my options, remembering the first step toward healing was being honest about the situation and openly asking for help. Counseling might prove helpful, or even medication when needed.

It took courage to start sharing my feelings with trusted friends. I purposely caught myself before giving an automatic response that I was "OK" or "fine" and answered, "Actually, I'm struggling quite a bit right now." And over this last month, I had shared prayer requests with multiple church and writing friends, hoping to lift the heavy mantle of despair. The gift must be from one of them—but who?

My husband came up the stairs and found me staring at the figurine. "Who sent you that?" he asked, unintentionally echoing my thoughts.

I looked over at him, wide-eyed. "I don't know! It was an anonymous gift. It's called 'Happiness'! It must've come from one of the friends I've talked with over the past couple of weeks. I wonder if there's any way I can find out who sent this without interrogating everyone," I pondered. "How can I write a thank-you note without knowing who sent it?"

"You can't!" he replied, stating the obvious.

I placed the beautiful figurine next to a vase of spring daffodils I'd rescued earlier from underneath the blanket of wet snow. The kind gesture had made me feel loved, but now the mystery of who sent the gift kept nagging at me.

The sender of this gift must have been one of those I'd confided in recently. If I could remember who I had spoken to, that would be a start to figuring out the mystery. My mind raced through my various friend groups. On impulse, I decided to jot down a quick list of friends whom I knew to be thoughtful or generous gift-givers.

At number sixteen, I laid the pen down, tears blurring my vision.

Sixteen? Sixteen! At least sixteen friends could have sent this gift, with still more I could add to the list! Oh, good gracious. Overwhelmed, I grabbed a tissue to wipe my eyes.

I realized right then that this was the real gift—that I could name so many good friends who might have made this sweet gesture. It felt both overwhelming and heartwarming at the same time.

I breathed thanks to God. This beautiful figurine was more than just a simple gift—it had pointed me toward a much larger treasure, one I knew would carry me through any dark days that lay ahead.

A Difficult Love
Jeanne Takenaka

My boyfriend Michael tried to tell me. He did—but I didn't pick up on his cues. We had just left my parents' home. They'd fallen in love with Michael. We laughed, told stories, and, unbeknownst to me, Michael asked them for permission to marry me.

I told Michael I looked forward to traveling and meeting his parents, which was when he said, "It will be . . . different . . . when you meet them."

I brushed off the caution in his tone. "I'm sure it'll be fine." How different could it be? They'd like me. I'd like them. End of story.

Our week with them birthed a complicated relationship. Within the first forty-eight hours, Bernard and Claire aired their opinions about abortion, politics, and religion. Opinions I didn't share. Because it didn't feel safe, I stayed quiet rather than express my thoughts—which led to critical words from Claire, who accused me of hiding something. I quickly realized building a relationship with them, particularly with Michael's mother, would require a lot of intentional effort.

When Michael proposed a few weeks later, I said yes. We married. Moving for Michael's jobs with the military, we made it a priority to travel to our families when we could. Each time we visited his parents, I made an effort to build a relationship with them, but it never seemed to be enough. As an example, early on in our marriage I attempted to help with cooking and dishes but was always dismissed. As Bernard and Claire aged, by necessity, I took over the kitchen responsibilities when we visited. Claire sometimes complained that I didn't sit to chat with them, instead cleaning up after meals. Verbal jabs easily spilled from her mouth.

Since I'm a person who experiences love through words of affirmation, Claire's unkind remarks cut deeply. Over time, those wounds festered. I wanted to show my mother-in-law respect without being emotionally vulnerable to her hurtful words and actions. My husband taught me a lot about what love looks like in how he listened to my hurts and supported me without dishonoring his parents. I sought to follow his example. I prayed for my in-laws and begged God for eyes to see Claire the way He did.

Several years into our marriage, my relationship with Claire hit a new low point. Michael, Bernard, and Claire decided his parents—who needed a house better suited to their aging bodies—would move into a new home. They would cover the down payment, and Michael and I would pay the monthly mortgage. Since we were paying the mortgage, it seemed logical to include my name on the deed. But this idea deeply upset his parents, particularly Claire. "If you die, she'll remarry and could sell the house out from under us. I talked with a friend. It happened to her." No matter how Michael tried to reassure his mother, Claire clung to this idea.

> **But if you do not forgive other people, then your Father will not forgive your offenses.**
>
> —MATTHEW 6:15 (NASB)

My mother-in-law's refusal to include me on the deed was a slap in the face to my character and my heart. After fifteen years of marriage, this was her opinion of me? Her accusation angered me. Michael and I had many conversations about how to navigate this roadblock. In the end, they acquiesced and did it Michael's way. We assured them they would live in their home as long as they were physically able or until they decided to move out.

But Claire's resentment carved out a chasm between us, and my bitterness began to fill it. As she sometimes did when she was not happy with me, Claire pushed me further away, almost to the point of snubbing me. There was no talking with her. No reassuring her I would honor the agreement, no matter what. I tried to show love for Claire in practical ways, but I couldn't invest my heart in a relationship with someone who maligned my character and intentions.

When she ignored my birthday, something she'd never done before, Claire's fresh insult drilled in even deeper the pain of rejection I had grappled with since I met her. We'd planned to meet his parents on a tropical Pacific island that summer, but the pain was so raw, I told Michael I didn't want to accompany him and our sons. Michael and I talked, and I did go . . . reluctantly.

I knew I needed to forgive Claire, but how does a person set aside heart hurts inflicted repeatedly over years? How do you forgive someone knowing they will continue to reject you?

I wrestled with God over these questions. He worked on my rejection issues.

The turning point for me was a conference where the speaker spoke truths I needed to hear. I had held on to unforgiveness for too long. The speaker told true stories of the work God did in people—physically, mentally, emotionally, spiritually—when they forgave those who hurt them.

I could no longer justify hanging on to the pain Claire had caused. I was a person of faith; Claire was not. God showed me that as long as I held on to past hurts inflicted by my mother-in-law and others, I could not live authentically in the present, and I couldn't represent faith in Jesus well. If I refused to forgive, past pain would always color how I viewed my present.

I had to come clean with God. I spent hours journaling. "God, I know I've held on to these hurts. Even though what happened is in the past, these words and actions still impact me. And it's built a wall between You and me. I don't want to live distant from You. I don't want to live with bitterness anymore. I want to live authentically and intimately with You."

And I wept.

> Therefore I, the prisoner of the Lord, urge you to walk in a manner worthy of the calling with which you have been called, with all humility and gentleness, with patience, bearing with one another in love.
>
> —EPHESIANS 4:1–2 (NASB)

No thundering voice boomed, "Jeanne, you are forgiven." Instead, a quiet peace like a breath settled in my heart. When I journaled about my experiences with Claire and I prayed about our relationship, my heart was grieved.

God gradually dismantled the stone wall around my heart. He enabled me to see her as He did: as a hurting woman who longed for control. She lived in fear of "What if . . . ?" Of imagined

Beloved *by* His Faithful | 89

outcomes, like the idea that if my name was on the deed to her house, I might be the ruin of her security. But even more, I finally saw that what she yearned for was love and validation.

We were two broken women who had disappointed each other.

Would Claire change toward me simply because I had chosen, at a heart level, to forgive her? Probably not. But her response was no longer my primary concern. Loving like Jesus became my primary desire.

A few years ago, Claire was diagnosed with breast cancer for the second time. No one expected her to live very long. Our family spent each Christmas with my in-laws because we never knew when their last holiday would be.

Claire still made cutting comments. At times, I still chafed, but God reminded me to shake off her words. Her opinion of me didn't determine my value. My lack of reaction to her barbs seemed to quell some of her need to put me down in order to build herself up.

In the last years when we visited Bernard and Claire, Claire's heart seemed softer toward me. Sometimes we would sit and chat. She related stories of growing up with immigrant parents. Of experiences as a young Army wife and some of the snubs she endured.

Understanding grew between us. Though she didn't say it to me, she shared her fondness for me with one of my sisters-in-law.

Sometimes we live out forgiveness by choosing to love and serve. Words don't always have to be spoken to confirm forgiveness has happened. In my case, Claire's gentling toward me, her choosing kind words, revealed her heart change. These changes freed me to express love to her in ways I never had in the past. I didn't recognize it at the time, but Jesus had been working in her heart longer than I knew.

GOD'S GIFT OF SIGHT
— Kim Taylor Henry —

WHEN PEOPLE THINK of the sense of sight, they usually think of perceiving something visible to their eyes. But there is another kind of sight that God uses, and upon which He places the most importance, as we read in Scripture: "The LORD does not look at the things people look at. People look at the outward appearance, but the LORD looks at the heart" (1 Samuel 16:7, NIV). Though we may lack God's infinite vision, we can follow His example and strive to see what is inside others as well as what is on the surface.

About a year before Claire passed away, while Michael was visiting her, she acknowledged Jesus as her savior. I would only see her once after that. We spent Christmas Eve 2020 on her back deck, sharing a meal, giving updates about Michael and our sons, and laughing with her as she regaled us with stories of her life.

Her health turned for the worse in 2021. Michael spent time with her in the hospital. Before she died, I had the chance to say one more time, "I love you, Mom." And I meant those words.

Her final words to me were, "I love you."

I cried hearing them.

Our relationship was not what I wished for when I said "I do" all those years ago. Hurtful actions and painful words ripped apart the fabric of that dream. The sewing together of two hearts came through the threads of forgiveness, of serving, of choosing to love when it wasn't returned, and of seeing Claire through God's eyes. It's only when we yield our hearts to Jesus that He can sew healing into the hurts we experience in our relationships.

A God of Miracles

Susan Shumway

I can't believe what just happened. Am I living in a dream or is this my new reality? How did I get here? The answer is simply God, His goodness, and His everyday presence in my life.

But let me go back to the beginning.

I had just accepted Christ in January of my senior year in high school, and that led me to a tiny Christian college on the east coast of Florida the following September.

I needed to find employment to help pay for school expenses, though. The area was filled with affluent people who employed college students to work for them, and I began to imagine myself getting hired by a wealthy family with a fabulous mansion. But I didn't have a car and could only apply to jobs close to school. So instead of working in that dream home—maybe near the beach or with a pool—I found a job at a nearby mobile home park for senior citizens.

The next year my sister gave me her car, which would come in handy even sooner than I'd expected. One day I was in the foyer of my dormitory when a friend walked in. She asked me if I needed a job, because the woman she worked for had a friend who needed some help.

When I arrived at the address for an interview, a delicate, beautiful woman opened the door. I had been terrified about the interview, but her smile and delightful demeanor put me at ease immediately. We talked, and I knew this was the woman I wanted to work for. Her husband was on the golf course, but the plaques and honors on the wall told me who he was—the recently retired CEO of a very large, well-known company. They were considering making Florida their permanent home. When I met him, I fell in love with his pleasing, kind disposition, too. I knew this was the job for me.

I worked for Mr. and Mrs. Parker for 3½ years, and we became very good friends. I *loved* my job, which made it difficult to really even call it a job. They had a beautiful condo filled with expensive things. When I went to their home, I felt I was in a different world, something that I had never experienced before. They were kind and appreciative and made me feel they were the ones indebted to me, which made me want to do even more to please them in any way. I could sense God's presence as I worked for them.

> "Father, I thank You that You have heard Me."
>
> —JOHN 11:41 (NKJV)

Mr. Parker asked me if there was any way I would stay on with them after graduation. They were building a large home and needed a full-time, live-in housekeeper. But I already had plans, so I thanked him and declined the offer.

Then, a month before graduation, my plans fell apart. After careful consideration, I told them I would return. It felt like God had orchestrated everything; He knew that the plans I had been pursuing were not right for me.

I moved in with Mr. and Mrs. Parker and took up my duties as housekeeper, which involved cooking and other household duties. The domestic world is my perfect setting, and my love for this couple and their admiration for me created an ideal scenario. Each morning, I would try to think of something I could do to make their day a little better. Their compliments and affirmations drove me to want to do even more.

This position ended when my boyfriend proposed to me, and we moved back to my home state to marry and begin our life there. However, the relationship with this very special couple continued, and we visited them and kept in touch. Sadly, one day I got the news that Mr. Parker was dying. I talked with him on the phone, and I will always remember that last time I heard his voice. His funeral was humble and beautiful, just what this influential man who had made a huge contribution to the world would have wanted. After his death, I continued to check on Mrs. Parker, and I visited her as often as I could. On one occasion, just as I returned home from a visit, Mrs. Parker's current housekeeper gave her two-week notice, and my old employer was beside herself. She needed to find someone for the three-month period before she went to her summer home. My husband and I decided that I should go to Florida and fill in until she could hire someone else. With a packed car, my children and I headed to Florida, which became home for us for the next three months. It was a joy for me to once again be with Mrs. Parker and help in any way she needed.

We returned home again, and a couple years later we got the sorrowful news that Mrs. Parker, who had been fighting cancer, was not doing well. One day her daughter Melissa asked her if there was anyone she wanted to see, and she asked for me. Melissa called me, and the next day I flew to Florida to be with Mrs. Parker in her final days. I felt honored to have been part of the Parkers' lives, and I felt God had certainly brought us together. It was a beautiful friendship.

After her funeral I returned home with a heavy heart. I had lost two people who had exemplified God's love through their lives and example. Kindness was always there, and I had never seen such a beautiful marriage.

Time moved on, and Melissa and I kept in touch. Previously, I had thought of her as the daughter of these two wonderful people, but as time moved on, she also became my friend. One day she called me from another state and asked if I could possibly help her with something for a 10-day period. My immediate answer was yes. I could see both of her parents in her, and I found joy in the times I would visit and get to know her even better.

At the time of my visit, I was ending an emotionally destructive marriage, and I was overwhelmed by all that entailed. I knew the divorce would put a real financial strain on me; however, it was something I had to do. Going to help her would give me a little time away to pray, reflect, and try to make some necessary decisions.

One morning I got up early to have some quiet time and read a devotional. It had a margin for journaling, so I began writing. I admitted to God that I felt I was drowning in all of the decisions that needed to be made. I told Him of everything that troubled me, from divorce to financial needs. Finally, I wrote, *God, I am overwhelmed with all of these things, but I know You have promised to care for me, so I give all of this to You.*

> "Ask, and it will be given to you; seek, and you will find; knock, and the door will be opened to you."
>
> —MATTHEW 7:7 (NKJV)

As I began preparing for breakfast, Melissa and I sat together and talked a bit about my current circumstances. I simply shared my story, then went about my day and didn't think any more about it.

That evening we once again had dinner together. She began talking to me about my situation and made a statement that changed my life.

"I've been thinking about everything you've been going through, and I want to help you in some tangible way." She mentioned a sum of money that she wanted to give me to help me through my divorce. "You cared for my parents 40 years ago, and I still remember the way my mother's eyes lit up when you walked into the room. I know what you did for my parents, and now I want to bless you for your love and care for them."

I broke down sobbing and tried to express my gratitude to God and to her. This was a modern-day miracle that would make an enormous difference in my life, and I knew God had orchestrated this from the very beginning of my time with her parents. "My marriage lasted 39 years," I told her, "and that whole time it was as if I was wandering in the wilderness. Now I'm about to step into Canaan." God's presence surrounded us.

It was almost exactly 12 hours after I had given everything to God. But then again, why should I be surprised? I serve a great God, and He came through with His perfect timing.

> **I have been young, and now am old; yet have I not seen the righteous forsaken, nor his descendants begging bread.**
>
> —PSALM 37:25 (NKJV)

The next morning, we were having breakfast again, and I asked her if I could read to her what I had journaled the morning before. After I read it, she simply and humbly said, "But Susan, if not me, then who?"

My life was forever changed. My faith in God hearing my prayers was affirmed in a greater way than I had even imagined. His presence is real. God works in mysterious ways, and He knew before I was created what my life held.

When the Strong Hit the Wall
Lynne Hartke

Hiking items covered the bed in our hotel room near the South Rim of the Grand Canyon. Backpacks. Water bladders. Bagels. Granola bars. First-aid kits.

We had already weighed and considered every item back home in Chandler, Arizona, but it was a ritual for us to always repeat the process at the hotel. We didn't want to carry one extra ounce on the rim-to-rim hike (R2R) in the morning, an almost 21-mile trail we planned to complete in one day.

We were joining a group of friends who hike the canyon every year. Although Kevin had made the hike a dozen times, I had hiked R2R only once before. I had not forgotten the difficulty of that experience.

We had trained for months, putting countless miles on our legs in preparation for the adventure. The hike consisted of approximately 7 miles down the South Kaibab Trail, 7 miles along the bottom of the canyon near the Colorado River, and 7 miles up the North Kaibab Trail.

As I stuffed a light jacket into my pack, I struggled with second thoughts.

Ten days earlier, I had developed a nasty sinus infection. Even with antibiotics I was unsure I was healed enough to participate. Then 3 days before the hike, I woke up with stabbing joint pain in my left hip, a new side effect from another prescription I was taking.

The doubts multiplied.

How will I handle the 21 miles in the canyon? The 4,720-foot drop in elevation from the South Rim? It's tough on the best days. Plus, the brutal 5500-foot gain in elevation to hike to the North Rim? Should I back out?

I weighed the options, listing the pros and cons. Kevin could hike without me, while I joined the shuttle drivers picking up the hikers at the end. Ultimately, I was afraid. I was afraid the hike would be too much. Too much for my muscles. Too much for my joints. Too much.

"I'll hike with you," Kevin said, as I rehearsed the options with him for the fifteenth time.

"What? No." I argued. "You planned to hike with the guys. You wanted to beat your best time." The guys had a tradition of recording their hiking times in a logbook, always striving to improve their speeds. I planned to hike with a slower group, stopping to take countless photos, while Kevin raced ahead.

"We'll hike together this time. Let's plan on it," Kevin insisted.

Relieved, I agreed.

> **Christ himself gave the apostles, the prophets, the evangelists, the pastors and teachers, to equip his people for works of service, so that the body of Christ may be built up.**
>
> —EPHESIANS 4:11–12 (NIV)

The next day, in the predawn morning, we hefted our backpacks onto our shoulders as we zigzagged down the switchbacks on the South Kaibab Trail. Our other friends quickly passed us. I counted seventeen switchbacks as we made our way down the rock layers of the canyon, including the Kaibab Formation, Toroweap, Coconino Sandstone, Hermit Formation, and Supai Group.

Although surrounded by layers of history, my mind shifted to earlier memories.

"Do you remember taking a photo with our kids at that lookout?" I asked. "Or how about the time we saw the bighorn sheep?"

"Or when we saw a condor soaring on the air currents," Kevin reminisced, naming the endangered bird that makes a home in the canyon.

As we hiked around bends and overlooks, I remembered other trips. Other photos. Other memories.

We had visited the canyon when icicles dripped from guardrails along the trail and when the temperature had soared over 100 degrees, making us long for a sliver of shade. We had carried toddlers under Ponderosa pines that smelled like vanilla. We had stayed at the canyon for a romantic getaway on Valentine's Day, just the two of us, and later as chaperones to out-of-town visitors who were catching a first glimpse of Arizona's largest tourist attraction.

The Grand Canyon was layered in our memory. The layers deepened the love and the tug that drew us back again and again. The one constant in the layering was the man who hiked beside me. I appreciated the fact that he could be up ahead trying to knock seconds off his best time as he raced down the trail, and yet he chose to hike with me.

A good relationship is found in the layering, I decided. Layers of memory. Of sacrifice. Of choices. Of walking together, side by side. Of good years—and difficult ones.

We had cared for my mother last year when she moved in with us at the end of her life. I appreciated the love Kevin showed her and how he had stepped in whenever I needed a break. I couldn't have done that difficult layer of our lives without him. I felt the same today.

"Look at that yucca," I said, pointing to a pointy-leaved succulent. "I need to stop and take a photo."

"Of course you do." Kevin smiled, aware of my photo-taking ways.

He waited patiently while I stopped to photograph a red-flowering claret cup cactus and the orange blossoms of a globe mallow.

"Let's take a food break," Kevin suggested when I finished snapping pics.

> **Therefore if you have any encouragement from being united with Christ . . . then make my joy complete by being like-minded, having the same love, being one in spirit and of one mind.**
>
> —PHILIPPIANS 2:1–2 (NIV)

"Are you sure?" I knew Kevin preferred to eat on the run, not wanting to slow down to consume calories.

"You will burn out if you don't take short stops," he said. Which was true. The layering had taught us these things.

I pulled out a bag of peanut butter–filled pretzels. "Do you want one?" I asked, offering him the bag.

"I'm good," he said as he munched on a piece of beef jerky.

Good was a great place to be, I decided, and settled into the moment. Kevin set his pace to match mine, conserving energy for the brutal ascent yet in front of us. After 7 miles of descending in layered stone, it was a relief to walk next to the Colorado River under the towering shade trees. At Cottonwood Campground, we refilled our hydration bladders with water and took another short break.

"Are you ready?" Kevin asked, slinging his pack over his shoulder. "Did you eat enough?"

I nodded and took another swallow of water. The final unending torture chamber of switchbacks awaited. Step over step, step over step, we plodded up the trail.

To deal with the exhaustion and to distract myself from my aching body, I focused on numbers. By the time we reached the Supai Tunnel, at which point there were almost 2 miles remaining, I was counting. One number for every four steps. Each time I reached twenty-five, I dug out a snack I had saved for this purpose—flavored jellybeans. The tiny treat provided a necessary distraction without taking too much energy for chewing.

23…24…25. *Brown jellybean. I hope it's not disgusting coffee. Ah. Root beer.*

23…24…25. *Orange jellybean. Tangerine.*

23 … 24 … 25. *Red jellybean. Cherry. One of my favorites.*

I had reached the zone where all that existed were numbers and bursts of happiness for my mouth. I wasn't aware of the scenery or other hikers, just counting and jellybeans. In fact, as I turned to head up another switchback, I realized Kevin wasn't with me.

I paused and waited. *Where is he?* Reality returned with the dawning sensations of a sore calf muscle and a dull ache in my hip.

I looked back and saw Kevin rounding the bend below me. He stopped and leaned heavily on his poles.

Without a word I knew he had "hit the wall," meaning he had expended too much energy and his muscles had seized up. From experience I knew his legs were filled with lactic acid and the only choices we now had were to sit down and sleep for several hours or gut it out with Frankenstein legs to the top.

I knew, also from experience, that I had just become the bride of Frankenstein.

As I waited for him to reach me, I wondered why he had hit the wall and I had not. Thinking back over the miles, I realized Kevin had been so careful to care for me, reminding me to eat and drink, that he had neglected to listen to the warning signs of his own body.

> **Carry each other's burdens, and in this way you will fulfill the law of Christ.**
>
> —GALATIANS 6:2 (NIV)

I thought back to my own experience of caring for my mom. To best care for her, I needed to be careful to take time and nourish myself. Kevin had stepped in multiple times to make sure I did that. We both knew even the strong can hit the wall.

Our roles reversed. As did the rock layers. Supai Group, Hermit Formation, Coconino Sandstone, Toroweap, and Kaibab Formation.

I slowed my pace to match his. We waited at the end of each switchback, taking a short break before beginning again.

"We made a new memory," Kevin said as we slogged our way up the final ascent to the trailhead where our friends waited with cold water and snacks.

"Together," I said. "We did it together."

Together was a good place to be.

Meeting God in Mama's Garden

Cheryl Wyse

As a young child, my grandmother and I often strolled hand-in-hand along the fragrant pathways of her summer garden. She told me that each flower represented a time of love and memory, a moment when she most keenly felt God's intimate presence. I felt it, too, as I held her hand and matched her slow and lingering pace.

We paused at each plant, her eyes glistening as she reflected on the loved one in her past who had gifted her with the bulbs and blooming bushes. Throughout her long life, friends and family remembered each of her many birthdays, anniversaries, and holidays with a gift that would show their love each summer as it bloomed. Each perennial became a visitor to my grandmother, evoking precious memories of its giver from years past.

"Each flower is a miracle in its own right," my grandmother told me. "Its annual bloom invites me to pause, spend time with God, and thank Him for His incredible wonders of life. Each flower is unique, as we are in God's presence."

My grandmother, whom I lovingly called "Mama," and I strolled and prayed throughout her garden, touching the gifted blooms, seeking God's blessings for those still living, and expressing gratitude for the givers who had passed. Even though a small child, I saw the cherished memories of those flowers reflected in Mama's face. Each sacred stroll deepened my understanding of the enduring love Mama held for God and for others.

Mama's garden didn't appear overnight. It began as a modest patch, a prayerful oasis she carved out of a dirt-dry space with a hoe, a dream, perspiration, and perseverance. The seeds, bushes, and bulbs rooted deeply into the soil, lifted their heads to the sun, and blossomed. A lilac bush held a special place in Mama's heart. It was a long-ago gift from her twin sister, a companion who grew close to her heart before birth and stayed close throughout her lifetime.

Over time, Mama's garden expanded. Yellow crocus and daffodils rose to welcome each spring, bluebells spread out a brilliant carpet beneath our feet, and hyacinths scented the air. Near the end of the season, peonies unfurled in red, white, and lilac, bidding farewell to spring and announcing the onset of a hot southern summer.

> **That person is like a tree planted by streams of water, which yields its fruit in season and whose leaf does not wither—whatever they do prospers.**
>
> —PSALM 1:3 (NIV)

Mama often paused and pointed to her favorite rose, the color of cotton candy. "Life is like this rose. There will be thorns, moments that hurt, but always focus on the bloom—the love, joy, and memories—that's what truly matters."

Little did I know then how this pink-bloomed lesson of wisdom would become a compass to help me navigate the inevitable storms ahead.

As her garden grew, so did I. I married a good man, then trekked with him to the heart of inner-city Boston. Our lives together became a grind of term papers, classes, exams, hard work, and all-night studies. The concrete inner city, overshadowed by fear, violence, and poverty, offered no patch of soil in which to plant a flower. In this stark landscape, I yearned for Mama's garden. For 7 years, I clung to the memories of our garden time together, remembering the truths she had taught me: "Even in the harshest conditions, faith can flourish, and God's presence can be felt."

> **Love is patient, love is kind. It does not envy, it does not boast, it is not proud.**
>
> —1 CORINTHIANS 13:4 (NIV)

During those years, Mama wrote me a letter each week, sharing her love and encouragement. The faithful letters—all 400 of them—became the sturdy bridge that connected me to her and to the long-ago lessons of her garden. I kept her handwritten letters, rereading each one when I most needed to feel her presence.

After graduation, we moved to Louisville, where I once again felt wrapped in nature, reveling in the Kentucky countryside's majestic old trees and cultivated flower gardens. We settled into life with a new job, a new home, and two pregnancies, the first steps in creating our family. I planted a small garden, filling it with the flowers Mama most loved.

While many dreams came true in those bluegrass Kentucky years, a particular thorn pained my heart.

One sweltering summer, pregnant with my second child and only days from her delivery, Mama left me unexpectedly,

GOD'S GIFT OF SMELL
— Kimberly Shumate —

THE FRAGRANT NIGHT phlox, or "midnight candy," is a flower that blooms in the cooler night air. Its tiny, cheery petals—some purple, some pink, some white—all open at the most unlikely time, even in the absence of the sun's light and warmth. Like the evening primrose and other night bloomers, their supremely fragrant smell is finest in its darkest hour. "Our lives are a Christ-like fragrance rising up to God" (2 Corinthians 2:15, NLT). Perhaps we delight Him best when our garden is tinged in darkness, yet our face still looks up.

---

making her way to meet the Lord she so loved. The distance between Louisville and North Georgia felt insurmountable. My doctor forbade me to travel, so I stayed home with my two-year-old son, missing the opportunity to say a final goodbye to my beloved grandmother. When my baby girl was born, I named her after Mama.

I wondered how I would live without Mama, my best friend, my spiritual nurturer, the one I had known and loved since my birth. But then I remembered her long-ago words: "Flowers have their seasons, just as we do—a time to bloom, a time to rest, and a time to begin again. It's God's way of teaching us about life, love, and eternity."

In the days and years that followed, I stepped often into my garden. The blossoms became my sanctuary, reminding me of the cycle of life—of endings and new beginnings. I felt Mama's presence, and I was reminded of God's presence, His unending strength and love that provided comfort in my time of missing Mama.

Now, as I look back over the many seasons of my long life, I regularly meet God in the beauty of my own expansive spring garden. As I take the hand of my young grandson, I am aware of how time has a wondrous way of weaving the past into the present. I see the same wonder in his eyes as I once felt in my own as we walk hand in hand along my own garden path. With each prayerful pause, I pass on to him Mama's wisdom and spiritual teachings.

Surely, the continuity of love and life stands as strong and as certain as the blooms that return faithfully each year. Passed down through the petals and prayers, I once again feel Mama's presence as my grandson and I bask in God's garden. It's a tender reminder that God is closer than our heartbeat and nearer than our breath, and that while seasons change, love remains, blooming eternally in the gardens of our hearts.

Grandpa's Priceless Gifts
Krystal Boelk

"He's gone." Dad choked on the words over the phone. My 98-year-old grandpa had slipped into heaven. I slowly folded onto the bed in my hotel room over 1,000 miles away while trying to catch my breath.

I could almost picture Grandpa lying in his room each evening, reading Scripture. He had always been a part of my life, even though I was now a mother myself and had lived far away from him for more than 20 years. My world would be incomplete, and a little scary, without Grandpa in it. He was my rock and safe place, as he was to everyone in my family.

Grandpa had been an important source of inspiration for my faith since I was a little girl. He frequently reassured me with statements like, "You can't out-give God, Krissy. You can't out-give God!" He didn't just say it, either—it was his way of life. He supported ministries dear to his heart, but this way of living really started right at home.

My earliest recollection of his generosity was when he used to pick me up from kindergarten and take me to River Oaks Restaurant in Kankakee, Illinois. He proudly made sure all the staff and other regulars knew I was his youngest granddaughter.

I'd make my request: "Oh Grandpa, I'm starving! Can I get the club sandwich?"

He'd reply, "Krissy, you will never eat all of that!"

My confidence won him over *every* time, and every time he ended up chuckling, saying, "Looks like your eyes are bigger than your stomach! You barely made a dent in it." He never made me feel ashamed for wasting food or for wanting an adult-sized sandwich. My feeling worthy of the sandwich was more valuable to him than a buck saved on the kid's menu. I never doubted that I was important to him.

I often asked him to tell me stories about his life. I felt as if his story was a part of me, like I was a part of him.

He told me about being the eldest of twelve kids and the impact the Great Depression had on them. "Mom would make dinner for us with just two potatoes," he would recall. His nickname, Mickey, came from his love of Mickey Mouse. His grandfather delivered the mail by horse and buggy, with Grampa as a helper as often as he was allowed. Grampa loved the horses, and eventually would own dozens of them in his lifetime.

He was a man with a childlike, pure, and loyal heart who joined the US Navy in 1941, and then sent home his wages to help his mom and dad quickly pay off their house. Knowing what he did reinforced my desire to follow his example and honor my own parents.

He wasn't one for praise or position. In fact, when we talked about his service medals from the Navy, he got choked up, saying, "Those boys who didn't make it home, they are the real heroes."

Grandpa and his brother, Clyde, were war heroes in their hometown of Momence. During World War II, when their ship, the *Hornet,* was hit by Japanese kamikazes and heavy artillery, they survived many hours of floating in the cold, shark-infested waters of the Pacific before they were picked up.

The memories of that time stayed with him forever. I could imagine how terrifying it must have been to watch bombs and planes come straight at you in the middle of the Pacific Ocean. Fourth of July fireworks always bothered him. And when we went to the beach, he would rather wait in the car than go sit at the water's edge of the beach, saying, "No thanks, I had enough of that."

We made great memories, even as he aged. When we were celebrating his 88th birthday at a restaurant near my home in Florida, the upbeat music made him grab me and lead me to the dance floor while he whirled me around. He loved to dance!

> **For this is how God loved the world: He gave his one and only Son, so that everyone who believes in him will not perish but have eternal life.**
>
> —JOHN 3:16 (NLT)

The fall before he passed, Grandpa and Dad spent a month at my home in Florida. While attending my home group Bible study, despite his dementia, Grandpa could still quote John 3:16 from memory: "Can you believe it? 'God so loved the world that he gave his only Son that whosoever believes on Him will not perish but have eternal life.' Isn't that something?" The group prayed a blessing over Grandpa. I was so touched, because I had never heard anyone pray for my grandfather before.

A month before he died, Grampa was still giving me strong hugs and assurance. "You know I love you, Krissy! Always have. Always will." And I loved him right back, my role model and inspiration.

When I went back home for Grampa's funeral, I longed to be in his space once again. "May I go in his room?" I asked Dad. "I would really like to have one of Grandpa's Bibles."

"Sorry, but I don't have one of his Bibles to give you. Your brothers already cleaned the room out," Dad answered.

I was deeply disappointed. I tried to let it go, but Grandpa had been so much a part of my life, and such a faith-filled inspiration, that I longed to have a Bible that Grandpa had held and read. I didn't know at the time that God was already at work—had been at work long before Grandpa even passed.

The year after Grandpa died, my husband and I were preparing to move to a new home. As we were going through the things in the attic, he gestured to a box and said, "I think one of your grandfather's Bibles is in there."

Curious, I opened the box. It was full of books, and I began to shuffle through them. My hand paused on one brown leather volume.

"Grandpa's Bible!" I shouted, taking the treasure in my hand. One of his Bibles had survived after all! I'd had a piece of him with me this whole time.

Tucked inside was a note written 20 years earlier: "Dearest Krystal—Please let this wonderful book always be your foundation in your life—and if you do—how great the rewards will be. Love ya girl. Gramp M."

Tears flowed down my face. How could I have forgotten this? At the time he had written that note, I had been a newly married military wife preparing for one of the many moves that my husband and I would make throughout our life together. I must have tucked the book into a moving box and then forgotten about it.

The fact that it had come back to me at all was a miracle of its own. My husband and I divorced in 2003, and this box of books was one that he took with him as he moved to California, then Illinois, then Michigan, and then to Florida when we remarried in 2015. God had kept that Bible safe all those years, through all those moves, knowing I would find this priceless gift at the right time.

> It is the same with my word. I send it out, and it always produces fruit. It will accomplish all I want it to, and it will prosper everywhere I send it.
>
> —ISAIAH 55:11 (NLT)

I would always miss Grandpa, but finding his Bible was a reminder of God's goodness, the way He watches over us even in the little things. I felt as if I was hearing Grandpa remind me once again to keep my life anchored in God's Word.

At the end of every day,
I look back at what
happened throughout my
day and I look for instances
of God's hand. This helps
me see that God's Hand
was always there—even
though I may not have seen
or recognized it when it
was happening.

—Monsignor Lloyd Torgerson

CHAPTER 4

Connected at the Right Time

Ordinary Faithfulness 116
   Laura Bailey

Stitched Together 121
   Courtney Doyle

He Will Not Let You Fall. 127
   Meadow Rue Merrill

Not a Moment Too Soon 132
   Wendy Klopfenstein

Connected in Mourning, Lifted in God's Love 137
   Jenny Leavitt

The Whisper of God. 144
   Tina Wanamaker

Ordinary Faithfulness
Laura Bailey

I'd been sitting in my car for the last hour, willing myself to walk through the church doors. I knew I couldn't avoid this conversation with my pastor any longer; I needed to share my feelings. Still, I couldn't shake the sense of dread.

With a deep sigh, I slowly unbuckled and shuffled into the church. I'd been serving as the women's ministry leader for a few years, so showing up unannounced and plopping myself on my pastor's couch wasn't that unexpected. Normally I came with a cheerful spirit, laughing and joking as I sat down, but today my sober mood immediately alerted my pastor that something wasn't right. In his usual gentle, calm way, he inquired, "What's wrong, Laura?"

I didn't get more than two words out of my mouth before tears began to pour down my cheeks. I was exhausted, frustrated, and overwhelmed by the demands of ministry. I felt like I was spinning my wheels. I'd invested countless hours planning, preparing, teaching, and mentoring the ladies of my church, but very little spiritual fruit was evident. I'd convinced myself that I was an ineffective leader and perhaps someone else would be better suited for the role. I would be stepping down at the end of the year, and he would need to start looking for my replacement.

While I'd only been serving in this particular role at the church for a little over a year, I'd been a part of the church and close friends with the pastor and his wife for nearly a decade. I'd voiced my frustrations to him before, so he was not shocked by my confession. After a long pause, he said, "You know that ministry is challenging, Laura. I am sorry you feel this way, and if you believe you need to take a break, I will support you. But know that just because you can't see big changes doesn't mean you've labored in vain and God isn't working."

A wave of comfort washed over me, and I was relieved that he wasn't disappointed in my decision. I took his words to heart, yet still felt I needed to take a step back. I left that meeting with a list of action steps, people to contact, and plans to put in place for the next women's leader. My decision to step down was final. Or so I thought.

Two weeks later, our church's music minister, Sandra—my spiritual mentor and friend to many—passed away unexpectedly. She was playing outside with her grandson the night before, everything as normal, preparing for Mother's Day the next day. And then, without warning, the Lord chose to take her from this earth, leaving her church, family, and community devasted. While we rejoiced and felt comfort that she was in the presence of her Savior, those left behind felt her absence profoundly. She did not achieve anything extraordinary by the world's standards, but I was overwhelmed by the stories of her love, kindness, and faithfulness to serving the Lord and His people that poured out after her death.

> **Therefore encourage one another and build each other up, just as in fact you are doing.**
>
> —1 THESSALONIANS 5:11 (NIV)

In the weeks after her passing, I replayed old voicemails, reread past texts, and rummaged through old cards and notes she'd sent me. She'd written numerous times over the past years to thank me for helping with an event, encourage me in my faith, or just give me a simple message of love and support during the birth of my girls.

But there was one card in particular that I lingered over. It read, "Don't stop believing in what God can do. Keep being faithful, as you are, serving Him; you are making a difference for the Lord at our church."

At the time, our church was going through a transition period. We were experiencing some intense growing pains. Attendees' general attitude was either apathetic or annoyed. Morale was low, and participation was almost nonexistent.

My husband and I hadn't been going to the church long. At only 5 years, we were relatively new members compared to others who'd gone to the church their whole life. But Sandra didn't care how long we'd been attending; she always made us feel like family. We became fast friends, and I started serving with her on various committees.

At the time, I was in my late twenties and spiritually and emotionally immature. I would quickly get frustrated in meetings, make biting comments without thinking, and give the cold shoulder or completely ignore people I thought weren't "worth my time." The irony was that I was just like some of the people I considered problematic who caused me to get so upset.

Instead of writing me off like I wanted to do to others, Sandra took me in with love, gentleness, and patience. I wasn't an easy student, yet she invested in my life, guiding and directing me to grow my faith and love for God's people—no matter how much they drove me crazy.

When they were looking for someone to start the women's ministry at our church, she recommended me and encouraged me to step into a leadership role. Over the years, the Lord has softened my heart, although my natural disposition is to run hot. I've learned to tame my tongue and control my temper, but I would often run to Sandra to unload my complaints. She would listen and allow me space to vent, but would always, in her soft tone, gently take my hand and say, "Just pray. You just have to keep praying. And Laura, sometimes you must love people for who they are, not what you want them to be." These were the last words she said to me the week before her death; as was usual, I was airing my grievances about something, and she responded as she always did.

As I sat on my bedroom floor, re-reading her words, recalling our last conversation, and thinking of Sandra's life, I felt the Holy Spirit speak to my heart through her words. I'd put limitations on God. In all my doing for the Lord, I stopped believing He could do more than I could ask or imagine (Ephesians 3:20). In this season of spiritual drought, I'd neglected my daily prayer time, and I surely wasn't loving people as Jesus did.

> **Never be lacking in zeal, but keep your spiritual fervor, serving the Lord. Be joyful in hope, patient in affliction, faithful in prayer.**
>
> —ROMANS 12:11–12 (NIV)

After reading that card, I knew the Lord wasn't calling me to give up as a women's leader but to give up trying to serve in my own strength instead of His. I went back to my pastor and

GOD'S GIFT OF TOUCH
— Linda L. Kruschke —

IN 1 SAMUEL 17, David was determined to face the giant Goliath, who had mocked Israel and their God. King Saul gave David his armor, but the armor didn't feel right to David. Instead, he "chose five smooth stones from the stream, put them in the pouch of his shepherd's bag and, with his sling in his hand, approached the Philistine" (1 Samuel 17:40, NIV). As he touched those smooth stones that fit perfectly in his hand, David felt and trusted the presence of God in his moment of need. Christians can use touchstones of their own to feel God's presence just as David did. What are some of yours?

---

told him I would continue in the women's ministry role, and since then I've worked hard to follow Sandra's example in my leadership.

It's been a little over a year since Sandra's passing, and I still tear up thinking about her and her impact on my life. The people who, like her, have had the greatest influence on me didn't win any great rewards, and likely won't be remembered for anything special, yet to me, their ordinary faithfulness inspired me in extraordinary ways.

Stitched Together
Courtney Doyle

My heart felt as though it had been torn into a million pieces. The pain wasn't physical like a heart attack, but it radiated through me just the same. Every breath felt heavy, as if my chest might collapse under the weight of it all.

It had been 6 months since life changed for all of us. Six months since I was able to physically hug my son and talk freely without our conversations being monitored. His absence in our family was felt by all of us, and to me it was a physical ache, a longing in my heart that never stopped. As if that wasn't enough, we were preparing to move our daughter to college 9 hours away. She was the first of our children to live so far away, and while in her case it was for a joyful reason, I knew her absence would leave another void in our lives. I was wrestling with how to navigate so many changes all at once. *Doesn't God see how hurt I am?* I wondered.

My husband and I filled our days with shopping, organizing, and all the other tasks needed to prepare for our daughter's move. Time was getting away from us, as was the list of "to-dos." Right now, the next item on the list was to take my daughter's car to get a tear in the seat repaired. My husband typically handles car-related issues, but we needed to divide and conquer before her final exit from Texas to Arkansas, so I was on "fix the car" duty.

I glanced back and forth between my map and the road. Highway 6 is a popular, well-traveled road lined with businesses, but four lanes of speeding traffic make it difficult to get to them, and I wasn't familiar with this area. Had I missed my turn? Frustration piled on to my already anxious, stressed, and broken heart; add "lost" to the mix and I was ready to throw in the towel. At last I pulled into what appeared to be the right shop.

The place had seen better days. Cars with missing parts were parked haphazardly around the lot. Loud music blared from what appeared to be the workshop, and a single rusty door greeted me as I approached my task for the day. *Where in the world has my husband sent me?*

When I walked through the door, I was greeted by two desks, piles of paperwork that surely belonged in the filing cabinets that lined one wall, and a chair that barely fit between the desks. There was zero room to roam. This wasn't an office—it was a closet with mismatched furniture, a worn leather chair, a computer, and a large desktop calculator. You know, the old kind with the paper roll. In the middle of it all was a man who greeted me with a friendly smile and introduced himself as Tim.

"How can I be of service to ya?" he asked politely.

> **Trust in the LORD with all your heart and lean not on your own understanding; in all your ways submit to him, and he will make your paths straight.**
>
> —PROVERBS 3:5–6 (NIV)

I explained he had spoken to my husband about repairing the seat in my daughter's car. I was simply here to drop off the car and get on with my very busy day.

We exited the "closet" together for him to assess the work that needed to be done—only for him to shake his head and inform me that they in fact could *not* simply stitch the leather back together; it needed to be replaced. Rather than the $75 that was previously quoted to us, now we were looking at more like $300. Rolling my eyes at this discovery and the sheer irritation of it all, I accompanied Tim back into the office and dialed my husband's number to let him in on our newfound expense. He was equally as irritated and frustrated as I was, and he said so loud enough for Tim to hear.

> **God is faithful; he will not let you be tempted beyond what you can bear. But when you are tempted, he will also provide a way out so that you can endure it.**
>
> —1 CORINTHIANS 10:13 (NIV)

I knew Tim could sense that this couple may just be at their breaking point. He was not wrong. It wasn't about the torn seat. It wasn't about the money. It was about another wave of unexpected chaos. The stress had been so consistent for so long that my husband and I were both struggling.

I ended the call and reluctantly told Tim to go ahead and fix the car. But instead of talking about timing or the fine details of the job, he sat back in his rickety chair and looked at me.

"You know, Proverbs 3:5–6 says . . ." He began quoting this verse.

"Why yes, Tim, I am aware!" I replied quietly, mostly so he wouldn't hear the nasty tone of my voice. I wasn't impressed. I thought to myself, *Good for you if you know a Bible verse.* Poor Tim! He had no idea what kind of turmoil had just entered his office. Looking back, I am not proud of how I acted.

One finger at a time, Tim slowly typed out the invoice while making small talk. At one point, he stopped his "pecking" to look at me and say, "You know, God won't give you more than you can handle."

Feisty me wanted to argue that statement, but poor Tim couldn't know what God had given our family, nor whether we were handling it very well. Back to pecking at the keyboard he went. Though I remained in that closet of an office, my patience had left the building.

Tim paused once again, turned his chair to face me, and apologized for his inability to quickly produce an invoice. "I'm the owner of this shop. The manager is on vacation, and he is much better at this computer stuff than I am. This isn't my full-time job. My full-time job is in prison ministry."

My heart stopped. *Did I hear him right? Prison ministry?*

My throat began to close. I swallowed hard, struggling to keep my voice steady as I asked, "Which prison?"

Like a little boy in a candy store, drawing his hands to his face with excitement, Tim told me the prison system he spent the most time in and then asked, "Do you know someone there?" He looked almost giddy with anticipation, sure that I did.

Chills ran through my body from the top of my head to the tip of my toes. For the first time in 6 months, I spoke the words that had weighed so heavily on me. "My son is in that prison."

I had told no one outside of my immediate family, yet here I was in a tiny office, on a road I never travel, irritated by the time and cost of a service, only to tell a stranger one of my deepest secrets.

"Drugs?"

"Yes."

Turning fully in my direction, sitting up straight, and looking me right in the eyes, Tim said confidently, "God is not done with him yet. You need to know there is hope. Do not give up. God has a plan."

This stranger began to share the story of a lost boy who ran away from home, turned into a drug addict, and spent all of his days involved in criminal activity to fund the addiction. At 40 years old, he was saved from that life and now serves the Lord in prison ministry. His name was Tim. He asked for my son's name and vowed to find him, pray with him, and give him a hug from his mom.

I walked back to my car in amazement, sat, and began to weep.

God was present.

He was there in my frustration, pain, sadness, impatience, anxiety, stress, and heartache.

He was present in an old, run-down car business that was aptly called "Stitches."

> **Give thanks to the LORD, for he is good; his love endures forever. Let the redeemed of the LORD tell their story—those he redeemed from the hand of the foe.**
>
> —PSALM 107:1–2 (NIV)

He was in Tim's life all those years ago.

He was in the prison with my son.

Several days later, the phone rang. My heart raced as I noticed on caller ID that the number was from the prison. I was anxious to hear my son's voice and hoping for good news, that today was a good day behind the walls.

"Mom, Tim found me."

For a moment, I couldn't speak. Tim, the stranger I had been so impatient with, had done something I couldn't. He had touched my son in a way that only God could orchestrate. My tears fell silently, and for the first time they weren't tears of sadness, but tears of hope.

Tim went on to meet with my son weekly, discussing Scripture and truth, and praying with him. That short but miraculous encounter with Tim, the stranger pecking at the keyboard and quoting Scripture, would make a lasting impression on my life and the lives of all those to whom I've told this story. Tim was present in his encounter with me. He saw I needed much more than a seat stitched together, and by doing so he taught me an important lesson: God is everywhere, and even when we may not be looking for Him, He is looking for us.

Through Tim's words and actions, God's presence came to calm my fears, meet my needs, and begin the process of stitching my heart back together.

He Will Not Let You Fall
Meadow Rue Merrill

I sat in the kitchen of our snug Maine fixer-upper, stressing about all I needed to get done before Christmas, just four short days away. With five children, my husband, Dana, and I never seemed to have enough time, but our lives were finally beginning to slow down. Our oldest two sons were grown and married. Our daughter, Lydia, was home from her third year of college. And our youngest sons, Asher, 13, and Ezra, 10, were excited to have a break from school.

As a middle- and high-school English teacher, I was ready for a break too. Forget the gift-giving and cooking. All I wanted was to curl up with a book and take a long winter nap, but first I had to find a recipe for the gingerbread houses I'd promised to bake with my boys that weekend. As I flipped through a cookbook, my cell phone buzzed. Picking it up, I read a message from a young father at our church. *Good afternoon,* his text said. *I was wondering if you are busy Saturday? Need someone to watch my kiddos for the day.*

Saturday? I sighed. Who wasn't busy on Christmas Eve? But God had put this single dad and his family in Dana's and my hearts. Earlier that year, he and his two preschool-aged children, Sissy and Bubba, had started attending our church. Bright and full of questions, the little girl reminded me of myself at her age. And her little brother was full of spunk, like my own boys had been. Sadly, their mother was no longer around.

In the short time we'd known them, the children's father had experienced significant problems, which cost him his job, followed by their apartment. Over the following months, he and his children had moved more than half a dozen times. First sleeping on family member's couches. Then moving into a homeless shelter. Then a tent. With support from our church, they were now back in their own apartment. Wanting to help, Dana and I had begun watching Sissy and Bubba several afternoons a month so their dad could rest.

The children loved playing with our two youngest boys, building block towers in the living room, digging in the backyard sandbox, and pushing each other up and down our driveway in my garden cart. But Sissy's eyes held a sadness that I recognized from my own childhood.

> "Don't be afraid, for I am with you. Don't be discouraged, for I am your God. I will strengthen you and help you. I will hold you up with my victorious right hand."
>
> —ISAIAH 41:10 (NLT)

Raised on an Oregon farm, I'd lost my father after my parents divorced when I was the same age as Sissy. My mother raised my older brother and me on her own, but our father's absence left an empty spot in my heart. Soon, my mom began taking our family to church, where I discovered the security I'd been missing. In songs and Sunday school stories, I heard about a God who loved me and who would always take care of me. I wanted to share this same love with Bubba and Sissy.

"God is always with you," I promised Sissy, holding her on my lap one day while Bubba played nearby. "He loves you, and wherever you go, He will take care of you. He will not let you fall." I reminded Sissy and Bubba of these words often, little knowing how soon God would test them.

So when I read their father's text, asking if I could watch his kids the day before Christmas, I texted back, *Sure. What time do you need us to pick them up?*

I'll be honest, he replied. *I messed up.* He revealed that after enduring so many hardships, he had suffered a setback. As a result, the state planned to take Sissy and Bubba into protective custody.

He will not let you fall, the words I'd promised Sissy so many times before, now echoed in my heart with probing clarity as I imagined Sissy and Bubba being sent to live with a family they'd never met. The loss of everything they'd known. If only we could help. But how? Dana and I both had busy jobs, and our three-bedroom house was bursting at the seams. We weren't even licensed to care for foster children.

> "So now I am giving you a new commandment: Love each other. Just as I have loved you, you should love each other."
>
> —JOHN 13:34 (NLT)

Even so, that evening at dinner I asked my husband and children, "What would you think about becoming a foster family?"

We all had concerns. How long would Sissy and Bubba be with us? How would we manage their school and daycare routines? And most concerning, what would happen if their father wasn't able to get back on his feet? We didn't have answers, but in a state riddled with addiction, Maine has so few foster families that children in custody are routinely cared for in hotels by social workers who come and go in shifts. Children have even been left in hospital emergency rooms, waiting for willing families to care for them.

So the next morning, I called the children's social worker and filled out paperwork to care for Sissy and Bubba. Because we already knew the children, we would be considered "fictive kin." Fictive, as in "fictional." Not real family, but close enough to speed up the process. To make room, our daughter Lydia gave up her bedroom and moved into my writing studio, a short walk down the driveway. Sissy and Bubba's grandmother, who was unable to take them full-time, offered to drive them to and from daycare. And friends helped Dana turn our front porch into a playroom. From car seats to childcare, our church and community and friends met every single need. Our pastor even delivered a toddler bed that her grandson had outgrown. Now all we had to do was pass our home inspection.

In place of Lydia's posters, I hung a picture of Jesus on the wall of Sissy and Bubba's new bedroom—the same picture of Jesus that my mom had bought for me when our family began going to church. The painting shows Jesus sitting in a garden surrounded by children. One little girl sits on his lap. As a child,

> **But Jesus said, "Let the children come to me. Don't stop them! For the Kingdom of Heaven belongs to those who are like these children."**
>
> —MATTHEW 19:14 (NLT)

I longed to be that little girl. Safe. And held. And loved. Praying that Sissy would feel the same way, I spread a pink comforter over her bed and made room for her and Bubba's toys on Lydia's bookshelf.

In all the excitement, Christmas came and went with little time to fuss over food and gifts. We completed our home inspection without a hitch. And on a rain-soaked night soon after, Sissy and Bubba arrived at our house with bags of clothes and gifts, many bought by our church.

If I thought I was busy before, I was even busier now. Particularly as Dana and I completed 1 month of training to become a licensed foster care family. In the process, we had to make a lot of adjustments. But after those first overwhelming weeks of medical appointments and classes and changes to our routine, our family has slowly found a new rhythm. One that now includes preschool swimming lessons, regular check-ins from the children's social worker, and weekly visits with their father, who recently started a new job.

It also includes bedtime stories, prayers and songs. "Jesus loves me, this I know," Dana and I sing to Sissy and Bubba every night before praying for their family. Propped on pillows, surrounded by stuffed animals and books, Sissy and Bubba join in. "Yes, Jesus loves me," they warble in their high, chirpy voices, pointing to their hearts. "Yes, Jesus loves me. Yes, Jesus loves me. The Bible tells me so."

Whatever the future holds, I pray that they will discover how deeply it is true. The same way we have. Because it is not just Sissy and Bubba who God will not let fall. It is each one of us. As we care for others, we too are safe, and held, and loved.

Not a Moment Too Soon

Wendy Klopfenstein

"Mom, I'm calling the doctor's office." I hated the stern tone in my voice as I stared at the thermometer. But she'd held off too long already.

Because Mom was a cancer patient, I had been instructed to call the nurse if her temperature ever climbed over 100.4. She'd not felt well the night before, but refused to let me take her in, insisting she'd be better in the morning. With the sunrise came a trip to the clinic for blood work. And a rising temperature. Whether or not she liked it, the time had come to go to the emergency room.

I put in a call to her doctor's office.

"We'll let the ER know to expect her. With her low immune system, she doesn't need to be waiting long in the general waiting area." The nurse reassured me before hanging up.

In a rush, my aunt and I packed a few things we might need, then got Mom into the car. Thirty minutes later, we pulled up in front of the emergency room entrance. Grabbing one of the available wheelchairs, we loaded her up. My aunt wheeled her inside as I parked the car then hurried to join them.

"Please sign in." The woman at the check-in went through the normal routine.

"Her doctor's office said they would call ahead to let you know she was coming." I offered the information while filling out paperwork. "She is a cancer patient, so her immune system is low right now."

After checking in, they directed us to the waiting room. We didn't expect to be waiting long. Usually, a call ahead from the oncologist meant a quicker response time.

Not that day.

An hour passed, then another. My mother grew pale, her exhaustion getting the better of her.

"There's a couch in the corner. Why don't I wheel you back there?" I eyed her weary face. "That wheelchair can't be comfortable."

She nodded. I wheeled her back to the corner by the window. In a matter of minutes, we had her moved to a more comfortable space where she could rest her head without slumping forward. In no time, a soft snore reached my ear. My aunt slipped over to the vending machines, and that is when I saw the cheerful face across the room.

Mom and I had been regular teachers in children's church until she became ill. Even when it wasn't her week to work, if they needed her, she went. She'd always offered a comforting smile and grandmotherly hug. The children loved her. And now one of the little girls from church came walking across the hospital waiting room to check on Miss Rita.

With a slow approach, she paused in front of me. "Is Miss Rita sick?"

> **And we know that in all things God works for the good of those who love him, who have been called according to his purpose.**
>
> —ROMANS 8:28 (NIV)

"She'll be all right." I offered what I hoped was a reassuring smile, then motioned to where her family waited. "I see your family is here with you. Is everything OK?"

The little girl nodded. By now, my aunt had returned to sit next to Mom.

"Why don't I go say hello to your mom?"

She grinned and held out her hand. I walked with her to the chair where her mother, Sharon, waited. Sharon explained that her doctor had sent her to the ER when her blood pressure rose.

"I guess it's just a precaution." Sharon's voice shook a little as she ran her hand across her pregnant belly.

"I'll be praying for you." I offered her the best answer I knew before hugging her and returning to my mom's side.

> **"For my thoughts are not your thoughts, neither are your ways my ways," declares the Lord.**
>
> —ISAIAH 55:8 (NIV)

Before long, the little girl found her way back to where I sat, bringing a tablet with her. She showed me her latest game. After a round or two, her family was called back to the exam rooms, and she hurried to join them. I waved as they left the waiting area.

I found it curious that they'd be called back first. They'd arrived at the emergency room long after us. My concern for Mom grew with each passing minute. Had they forgotten her somehow?

Just then, a nurse called from the front of the room. "Rita."

Mom gave a start. My aunt and I helped her back into the wheelchair, then I wheeled her back to the exam room. Once there, her chills increased.

"How long have you been waiting?" A nurse furrowed her brow.

"Over two hours," I said.

"That's unusual for a cancer patient." She shook her head, then went on with her duties.

After a few tests, along with multiple doctors and nurses coming and going, they had an answer. Sepsis.

"If you'd waited any longer, she might not have made it." The ER doctor spoke in low tones. "But we think we've found the source of the infection. We'll keep her overnight in the ICU."

Overnight turned into a week-long stay at the hospital. My sister and I took turns staying with Mom. During that time, I learned that Sharon had given birth to a baby boy. She was on another floor of the hospital. Once my sister and I had the all-clear that Mom had nothing contagious, we went to visit Sharon and her new baby.

> **Trust in the L**ORD **with all your heart and lean not on your own understanding.**
>
> —PROVERBS 3:5 (NIV)

After exiting the elevator on the maternity floor, we located Sharon's room number and knocked.

"Come in." Her voice carried sweetly into the hall.

"Hello. It's us." We rounded the door to see her sitting up in the hospital bed.

"My first visitors from the church!" A grin lit Sharon's face. She explained they'd admitted her with pre-eclampsia, and the situation had called for her to have her little one without delay. "I was worried. But when I saw you and your mom in the waiting room, I somehow knew everything would be OK." Her smile spoke volumes. "It was an answer to prayer."

Beloved *by* His Faithful | 135

After holding her new little one, I left with a sense of awe. I couldn't wait to tell Mom. Even in an ER waiting room, Mom was still ministering to others. Only a miracle could have placed us all in the right place at the right time. The little girl's mother received the reassurance she needed, as well as the medical attention. And Mom received her care. Not a moment too late and not a moment too soon.

Connected in Mourning, Lifted in God's Love

Jenny Leavitt

I first met Linda on a warm Florida morning at the high school where I worked as a secretary. She was trying to enroll her daughter, but seemed disoriented, looking around as if she wasn't quite sure what she was trying to do. I could sense the heaviness in her eyes and a weight that mirrored the sorrow that I carried within my heart. As our eyes met, a silent understanding passed between us. After a brief exchange of pleasantries, she confided in me that she had lost her son 3 weeks ago—a vibrant young 17-year-old who had been due to graduate high school in 2 months, taken too soon in a tragic accident.

Her voice quivered with emotion as she shared snippets of her story. I could feel the ache in her words, the raw pain of a mother's shattered heart. Listening to her stirred memories of my own loss.

I reached out and patted her hand, feeling the weight of her grief resonate through me. "I lost my son, too," I shared. "Even though it was a few years ago, the pain never truly goes away. Here's my name and number. If you ever want a friend, I'm here for you."

Her face lifted for a moment. We stood in silence, two mothers bound by loss and a flickering hope that they had found someone who understood.

Later that same day, my phone rang as this newly bereaved mom reached out to me. Emotions surged as I recounted our own family story.

"If you're up for it," I said, "I would love to meet for lunch sometime."

"I would really like that," she told me.

One sunny afternoon, not long after, Linda and I sat on an outdoor patio overlooking a lazy river nearby, sipping iced tea. The warm breeze carried the scent of the marsh, while the chatter of the birds and the rustling of the reeds provided a soothing backdrop for our conversation.

"I miss him so much," she whispered. Tears welled as she continued, "Every day feels like a struggle."

"The pain of losing a child is a pain like no other," I replied. "A friend told me it's like joining a club that no one wants to join. Once you're in, you can never leave."

She nodded, her voice breaking. "I just hope he's at peace. He didn't die instantly."

Heart breaking, I tried to gather my thoughts about how to respond. We'd chatted enough at this point that I knew she was not a Christ follower as I was. I wanted to be sensitive while also trying to help share the burden. *How hard it is to offer someone the hope of seeing their loved one again when they don't have the hope of eternity themselves,* I thought.

Before I could formulate a reply, she visibly shook herself, brushing a tear from her cheek. Straightening her spine, she said, "I just need to be strong. I've had losses before and survived. I will survive this."

I was hesitant to ask her if it was OK if I prayed for her, but it was the response that kept coming into my mind. To my surprise, when I did ask, she immediately said, "Oh, yes, absolutely. I would also really like to keep in contact with you if that's OK, Jenny."

It was my turn to say, "Oh, yes, absolutely. Please do."

Later that night, I couldn't shake the thought of how I would respond if she asked me the question that I dreaded: is my child in heaven? The uncertainty of how to approach this sensitive topic filled me with apprehension.

As the days, then weeks, passed, our conversations deepened, weaving a bond of understanding and empathy between us. She spoke of her son with a mixture of sorrow and pride, recounting the moments they'd shared and the dreams he'd harbored in his heart for his future. I listened,

> **May your unfailing love be my comfort, according to your promise to your servant.**
>
> —PSALM 119:76 (NIV)

offering a shoulder to lean on, all the while grappling with the subject that weighed heavily on my heart and wondering what I would say if she broached the topic of eternity. It seemed like the unspoken question hung in the air begging to be answered: *Where are our children now?*

I know who I put faith in. And thank God, I know my son had experienced his own come-to-Jesus moment. God has been gracious to our family and left behind clues that our son made his peace with God before he met Him face to face.

So, in the quiet of my home, I earnestly sought God in prayer, pouring out my need for wisdom. I made a choice to share my son Jacob's story with Linda, to offer her a glimpse

Beloved *by* His Faithful | 139

into the enduring love of God and how He covers our children with that love. Even in the darkest of times.

Just four days after we lost Jacob, while sorting through some of his paperwork, I had found a handwritten poem. It surprised me, because he was not a poet. His composition, *Holding Me*, is a portrayal of his wrestling-with-God moment. He admits to being a sinful man and wondering how God could ever use him. Then the tone changes, and he realizes the depth of God's love and accepts His graciously offered forgiveness. Peace floods over him. He confidently declares that the Lord has held his hand all the way. He knows there is no turning back. In the last two verses, he talks about meeting his Savior face to face and dancing on streets of gold.

He had signed and dated it with a flourish: *Jacob Leavitt, February 2015*. Jacob penned those words just 6 months before the Lord called him home. It still inspires a sense of awe in me to know the length that our God goes through to reach our children.

While I waited for an opportunity to share Jacob's story with Linda, we continued to connect via text or a quick meal when we could. But at the back of my mind, I still wondered when she would bring up the question of where our children were now. Our conversations had been skirting around Christianity, faith, and even eternity, but nothing direct. Yet.

Then one day, all thoughts fled my brain as she said with trembling emotion, "Jenny, did you know my son used to spend summers helping run charter boat excursions with a captain who was a devout Christian?"

"I don't think you've shared that with me before."

She continued, "Yes, he loved the water, and the captain had a very positive impact on my son's life. They shared a special bond."

I felt a stirring in my soul, a sense of anticipation building within me. Could it be that God had planted seeds of faith in her son's heart through the captain's influence?

Her eyes searching mine, she continued, "Well, the captain called me recently and told me something that took me by surprise. He said that last summer he prayed with my son to receive Christ and even baptized him in the Atlantic Ocean."

Wow.

"That's wonderful!" I said.

It had now been over a year since her son passed. I asked, "I wonder why he just now called you?"

> **I consider that our present sufferings are not worth comparing with the glory that will be revealed in us.**
>
> —ROMANS 8:18 (NIV)

"He said he didn't want to offend me, since he knew we weren't churchgoers. But he felt deep in his heart he was supposed to let me know."

My heart overflowed with gratitude and awe as God's perfect plan unfolded before us. The pieces of the puzzle fell into place, revealing the intricate ways in which God had worked in her son's life.

Tears glistened as she added, "Knowing that my son decided to follow Christ brings me a sense of peace that I can't describe. It's like a weight lifted off my shoulders."

I reached for her hand, squeezing it gently. "God works in mysterious ways. He had a plan for your son. A plan that involved the love and grace of Christ touching his life in ways that we will never fully understand. And to think—we may not have ever known that if the captain hadn't shared it with you."

A sense of peace descended on us, a tangible presence that enveloped us with its warmth and comfort. In that moment, I knew without a doubt that God's timing and presence were clear in our lives, guiding us to be instruments of healing and hope for those in need.

> **The LORD is close to the brokenhearted and saves those who are crushed in spirit.**
>
> —PSALM 34:18 (NIV)

In the days and weeks that followed, we leaned on each other for support and strength. We spent hours talking and reflecting on the incredible ways in which God brought us together. Our friendship deepened. Then, one Sunday morning, she walked into church! I had the privilege of leading her to Christ as tears streamed down both of our faces.

Embracing me, she said, "Thank you for being here for me. For sharing your faith with me. I don't know where I would be without you."

"It's not me," I replied, holding her close. "It's God's love working through us, guiding us and comforting us in our time of need."

Our faith continued to strengthen together as our friendship blossomed on a whole new level. Hearts filled with gratitude for the divine appointment that led us to each other as I witnessed a glimmer of light in the darkness of her life. A sense that maybe, just maybe, there is hope after all.

As the months passed by, her heart began to heal. The wounds of loss slowly scabbed over, leaving behind scars that spoke of love and remembrance rather than pain. We attended church together, prayed together, and lifted each other up in

GOD'S GIFT OF HEARING
— Lawrence W. Wilson —

WHICH CREATURES HAVE the best hearing? Bats can detect high-pitched sounds up to 200 kilohertz, which allows them to navigate by echolocation. Some whales can hear sounds as low as 16 hertz, which enables them to communicate across long distances under water. Humans generally hear sounds between 20 hertz and 20 kilohertz. That's better than dogs on the low range, but worse in the higher frequencies. However, it allows hearing of the human voice and sounds indicating danger without the distraction of less useful sounds, which become noise. It appears that God created each creature with hearing according to its need—and us with the ability to hear His messages in the world around us, even if we sometimes need a little prompting.

---

moments of weakness and doubt. Our faith grew stronger, our hearts more resilient in the face of tragedy.

All because God intervened in our lives in the most miraculous of ways.

We remain close friends, bound by a shared experience of loss and redemption. The pain of losing our sons never fully left us, but we turned it into a well of strength, becoming a source of compassion and understanding for others who walk the same path of grief.

The Whisper of God
Tina Wanamaker

I pressed the button to end the call and then sat for a moment to process what had been shared. Abby, my friend Shelly's daughter, had called to tell me that if I wanted to say goodbye to her mother, I should come to the hospital now.

My friend Shelly had been battling cancer for several years. She would go into remission and then after some time be told the cancer was back. This time, it wasn't looking good. I had eaten lunch with her at an Italian restaurant about a month before. She shared her concerns about how her family would handle things when she was gone. She knew her time was limited.

She had a request for me: to share the gospel with a group of her friends. She wasn't sure if they knew the Lord. Her desire was to invite certain ladies to her house and have me come and share with them. Shelly wanted to make sure they had heard about Jesus and what He had done in a very clear and direct way. She listed off some of the ladies she wanted to attend and told me she would contact me when she had it set up. I told her I would be happy to fulfill this request for her.

I left the restaurant that day not knowing it would be our last conversation. About 2 weeks after our lunch, Shelly took a turn for the worse. She was never able to schedule the meeting she was hoping to have. Now she was lying in a hospital bed with folks coming to say their goodbyes—including me.

At the hospital, I greeted Shelly's children, then headed into her room. Shelly was non-responsive. She was wearing a knit beanie cap to cover her hair loss and laying peacefully in bed. She looked so small. I reached down and took her hand and held it for a time without speaking. And then I leaned down and whispered in her ear, "I'll see you in glory, sister." There were more people waiting to see her so I quickly prayed with another lady there and left. Shelly went to be with the Lord later that day.

Her funeral was planned by her family. As the day approached, I began to consider Shelly's request. I had been talking with the Lord about it and came to the conclusion that I should honor her desire and have the meeting, even if she couldn't be there with us. I asked the Lord how to go about this as I didn't know the ladies who had been listed to me by Shelly. I felt I should ask the Lord for a connection at the funeral, for Him to bring someone who could help put this together.

> **"Indeed these are the mere edges of His ways, and how small a whisper we hear of Him!"**
>
> —JOB 26:14 (NKJV)

The day of the funeral came, and I arrived at the funeral home. The service was lovely. Following the service, we went to the burial site and back again to the funeral home for the reception. I sat down next to a woman named Connie and began a conversation with her. After a bit, I told her that Shelly had made a request of me that I wanted to fulfill. As I explained what Shelly had wanted me to do, Connie sat quietly, listening intently. She leaned over and said, "I know all of these ladies, and I can help you contact them." The Lord had brought His connection. We exchanged numbers with the promise to be in touch.

A few days after the funeral, I heard from Connie. She sent me a list of phone numbers and told me that each woman was agreeable to being contacted by me. I contacted each of the five women on the list and explained Shelly's request to have a meeting to share something that had been put on her heart. They each said yes, they'd like to be involved. After this, I began to ask the Lord for His timing. When should I have the meeting and where?

As I waited on the Lord for this, things began to become clear. It seemed good to have the meeting in a small event space in a local coffee shop. There was also a specific date that seemed right for it. The date puzzled me a little, as it was a Thursday evening. But I had asked for and received direction, and therefore stepped forward into that. I rented the room, sent out the date, and began to pray for the meeting itself.

The appointed Thursday evening came. I sat in the rented space alone, wondering what God had in mind. As the women came, one by one, I greeted them with a hug. The six of us sat there together, joined by bonds of love and grief, and began to share about our friend. First one, then another, until everyone had shared something of their relationship with Shelly.

I told the ladies of Shelly's desire to have this meeting. I shared from my heart what Shelly had wanted me to tell them: That she had specifically named each of them. That she loved them so much she wanted to make sure they had clearly heard the good news of the gospel. I explained the hope she had and spoke of her final destination. The women listened, and it turned out some of them already fully understood, while to others it was new. We prayed together.

Our time together was coming to an end, but one woman, Esther, had something she wanted to share before we left. Each year on her birthday, Shelly would take her out to do something. Esther didn't have any family to celebrate with. Shelly knew this and became the one who year after year would remember and make sure she had something to look forward to on her birthday, whether it was dinner or an outing. With Shelly now gone, Esther hadn't known what she would do for her birthday.

Then Esther leaned forward and said, "Today is my birthday." I was quiet as what she said registered. Today was her birthday—the very day the Lord had led me to arrange this gathering. I had been puzzled by the date, but now I understood. The Lord was showing His great care for Esther. He wanted her to know that He was with her, He saw her, He knew her. Each of us teared up as we caught a glimpse of God's hand.

> **The steps of a good man are ordered by the LORD, and He delights in his way.**
>
> —PSALM 37:23 (NKJV)

The women left, one by one, the same way they arrived—with a hug. When all had gone, I opened a card left by Esther.

It detailed how much the timing of the meeting had meant to her. In honoring Shelly's request, we had each seen a whisper of God. We had seen a small sampling of how big He is, how much He cares for each of us individually, and how involved He is in the details of our lives. The Lord had laid a burden on Shelly's heart and she had shared that with me. After she was gone, He had led me to complete what He had begun. And in doing so, I was given a firsthand seat to His handiwork.

We are a community. . . .
Our individual fates
are linked, our futures
intertwined. And if we act
in that knowledge and in
that spirit, together, as the
Bible says, we can move
mountains.

—Jimmy Carter

CHAPTER 5

Community of Caring

Finding Family Far from Home................150
    Vicki Bentley

How Friends Filled a Father's Void..............156
    Amy Hagerup

Miracle after Miracle......................162
    Robin Ayscue

The Hope Chest.........................168
    Renee Mitchell

Struck Down but Not Destroyed...............172
    Joanna Eccles

What Matters Most.......................177
    Stacey Thureen

Calming the Storm Clouds 181
    Peggianne Wright

Whole Again 187
    Tammy Gerhard

Finding Family Far from Home

Vicki Bentley

"What do you mean you have to leave?!"

The moving van parked in the driveway of our new home was still almost three-quarters full, yet inexplicably, the movers we had hired to help us were packing up to leave. "We have to get to another job," one replied with a dismissive shrug of the shoulders. "There's nothing we can do."

Staring at the mountain of stuff we still had to move and set up inside, I wanted to cry—much like the wailing 6-month-old on my hip. With only my husband and me to finish the job, it would take us hours. But as I collected myself and said a silent prayer, I was reminded of the truth that God had been whispering in my heart every time I felt alone: "Do not fear. I am with you."

Smiling shakily at my husband, I took a deep breath. "We can do this. But we're going to need to make some calls . . ."

When our plane first touched down on the east coast of America, 3,000 miles from our family, friends, and church community back in Scotland, I couldn't help but wonder if we had made the right decision. *Are we sure this is God's will for us in this season? Will we ever grow roots that are as deep and rich as the ones we just left behind? Will this new country and culture ever fully feel like home?* The answers to my questions weren't forthcoming; nonetheless, I held on to the knowledge that God promised He would be with us on this journey every step of the way.

As my husband and I disembarked from the plane into a new country and a new life, I clutched on to this truth like a scriptural security blanket, covering me with peace. God was with me, and while nothing else in my life was certain, I could count on Him.

In those early few months, I felt unmoored. With hours to kill while my husband was at work, the days felt long and lonely, and I longed for a friend to help me bridge this transition. Suddenly lacking the steady foundations I had taken for granted back "home," I turned to the only sure foundation on which I could stand—the solid rock of Christ. He hadn't changed. He was still with me. And I could rebuild my life upon Him.

We knew we desperately needed a community of believers around us to hopefully stand in the gap for us in this new season, so finding a church to call home was at the top of our agenda. We felt prompted to attend Grace Fellowship—a large church in a former strip mall that was right next door to our apartment. It was bigger than we had hoped, and we worried about getting lost in the crowd; however, our fears were

> **"The LORD himself goes before you and will be with you; he will never leave you nor forsake you. Do not be afraid; do not be discouraged."**
>
> —DEUTERONOMY 31:8 (NIV)

unfounded, and we were warmly welcomed. To our astonishment, we were quickly connected with another couple our age who were not only from Scotland but also lived in the same apartment complex as we did. What were the odds? This happy coincidence felt like a warm, comforting hug from the Lord—a tangible reminder of His presence manifesting through His people. It was a gift to have a friend living practically next door who was able to relate completely to my situation, introduce me to the area, and provide much-needed company in those early months while we settled in.

My husband and I also took the plunge and joined a small group at our church with several other young couples. From the first moment we stepped into the home of the couple that led the group, met by the inviting aroma of coffee and banana bread, it felt like we belonged. As we continued to have regular fellowship together—sharing what was happening in our lives and studying God's Word together—acquaintances blossomed into strong friendships. It took time and effort to grow these foundational relationships, yet we could see God's hand in it all through the way He was positioning His people around us. Slowly but surely, He was building us a community we could call our own. He was making good on His promise.

A few years after our move, I was thrilled to discover I was pregnant with our first child. While I couldn't wait to begin this exciting new chapter, as a first-time mom thousands of miles from home, I felt no small amount of trepidation. *How will my husband and I cope with our parents so far away? Can we really do this on our own?* However, as I surrendered my fears to God, He firmly but gently reminded me that I wasn't on my own. I never had been. His constant presence had been with me every step of the way, and He wasn't going anywhere now.

I trusted that He would provide us with the support that we needed when it mattered most, and He didn't let me down. A few weeks before my daughter was born, the ladies from our couples' small group at church threw me a surprise baby shower. As they prayed over my baby girl, tears of gratitude flowed freely. What a gift to have this unyielding support from women of faith I had only known for a relatively short time.

I was blown away by God's goodness and grace toward me—and He wasn't done yet.

In the early months of motherhood, I felt as though I was drowning. My daughter, who was later diagnosed with autism spectrum disorder and ADHD, was not an easy baby, and I struggled with establishing a routine.

> **For no one can lay any foundation other than the one already laid, which is Jesus Christ.**
>
> —1 CORINTHIANS 3:11 (NIV)

It was a blessing when my small group set up a meal train during those difficult few weeks until my parents arrived to help. The Moms Offering Moms Support (MOMS) ministry at my church was also a lifeline in a hard season, offering a warm and welcoming place to connect with other moms and drink from the refreshing water of God's Word—and a strong cup of coffee! These new mom friends rallied around me—and one another—as we navigated those overwhelming early few postpartum months. We bonded over our endless questions, doubts, fears, frustrations, and simple joys, and the knowledge that I wasn't alone in this exhilarating, exhausting journey was a balm to my soul, bringing peace and gratitude to my heart. It felt as though I had truly found my people, as God promised I would.

Six months later, as I stood on that baking hot August afternoon in front of our new home, I shouldn't have worried. Not half an hour after we started making calls, the cavalry arrived. Friends from our small group at church and the MOMS ministry, plus a few others whom we served alongside in the youth ministry came ready to work. Before long, the van was empty, and there was even a team to assemble our daughter's crib. My heart almost burst with gratitude at the effort they were making on our behalf and the way they had selflessly given up their time and energy to help us in our hour of need. It was a beautiful representation of the selfless servant heart of Christ, and once again, I thanked Him for bringing this community of believers into our lives in a season when we needed them most.

> "For I know the plans I have for you," declares the LORD, "plans to prosper you and not to harm you, plans to give you hope and a future."
>
> —JEREMIAH 29:11 (NIV)

Nine years have passed since that memorable day, and my family and I are still part of the same church community. While the original couples' group we attended eventually ran its course, the friendships remained. In fact, the woman who first hosted us in her home is now a dear friend and godmother to my two daughters. Many of the friends that were made at the MOMS ministry have also

GOD'S GIFT OF SOUND
— Terrie Todd —

EMPTY-NESTERS WOULD AGREE the most beautiful sound in the world is the laughter of their adult children gathered together. Having endured years of bickering, hearing our offspring enjoying each other sounds like a symphony. Imagine the joy God feels when He hears the laughter and camaraderie of all of His children, regardless of where they grew up. When those children acknowledge His presence in their midst and include Him in their party, He rejoices, as we hear in Zephaniah 3:17, "The Lord your God is with you. . . . He will take great delight in you; in his love he will no longer rebuke you, but will rejoice over you with singing" (NIV).

---

become like family, and it's been a blessing to see our children grow up together through the years and now embark on their own journeys of faith. Throughout the years, there have been Bible studies, book groups, babysitting swaps, camping trips, and birthday and holiday gatherings. This community that God created for us has laughed and cried together, celebrated with and carried one another, but above all, has been there for one another. Ministering to us in our loneliest hour, they have been, and continue to be, an enduring reminder of God's constant presence, no matter where we find ourselves and how far we are from home.

How Friends Filled a Father's Void

Amy Hagerup

Christmas can be a magical time for children, with visions of sugarplums dancing in their heads. But it can also be a time of intense anxiety for a stay-at-home mom dependent on her husband to make her children's Christmas dreams a reality. That is what my mother experienced when I was nine years old.

The year before, when I was eight years old, I remember my three siblings and I watching for Daddy to arrive home on Christmas Eve. When he drove into the driveway, we could see colorful striped dowels through the car windows, and we jumped up and down together. He opened the driver's door and yelled, "Get away from that window!" We quickly obeyed, but his anger didn't dampen our excitement.

Christmas morning revealed a pink-and-blue doll bed for my little sister—that crib sported the dowels we had seen through the car windows. We three older kids were swooning over our new bikes. Our large stuffed animals took up proud positions on our pile of presents and filled stockings, but I noticed that there was no present for Mama from Daddy and thought that was strange.

Then, a few months into the new year, I became aware that things were different at home. Sometimes, when we would gather around the red Formica table for supper, Daddy's chair would be vacant. When asked where he was, Mama said she hoped he would be home soon. During our prayer time, she prayed that he would come home.

One night, when I got up to go to the bathroom, I saw Mama kneeling in front of the couch. When I glanced into their bedroom, I noticed that Daddy still wasn't home.

Mama would whisper on the phone to her friends from church. I think they knew what was going on in my parents' marriage. One time, when I needed to ask Mama a question, she didn't see me standing behind her. I heard her say, "JoAnn, I don't know what I am going to do. George hasn't given me any money for groceries." I gasped a little when I heard that because I had noticed the fridge was empty. The other day, we had had hot dogs for breakfast, which I thought was strange, but they were yummy, so I didn't mind.

Then Daddy would come home again, and we would all go to church together, where he was the minister of music. Mama played the piano, and they often sang duets together, harmonizing beautifully: I can still hear them singing "Tis So Sweet to Trust in Jesus."

However, that harmony didn't carry through at home. On Monday night, Daddy's chair at the dinner table would be empty again.

> "The King will reply, 'Truly I tell you, whatever you did for one of the least of these brothers and sisters of mine, you did for me.'"
>
> —MATTHEW 25:40 (NIV)

Mama started teaching piano lessons to her friends' children. Although her college degree was in education, she couldn't get a public school teaching job until she renewed her certification. She had not been in the workforce since my oldest sister had been born eleven years earlier. Mama's piano lessons provided her with some income so she could buy groceries.

The months continued to click by until December finally arrived. Christmas would be here soon. My siblings were eleven, seven, and three; I was nine. We all sat at the window again on Christmas Eve, watching for Daddy's car, but he didn't arrive before bedtime. When Mama kissed me good night, I heard her sniffling and saw her wipe her eyes. *Maybe she's getting a cold*, I thought. I wasn't sure.

When I was an adult, my mother told me what had happened that somber night. It was very late when my father drove into the yard and came into the house empty-handed. Mama was devastated. She asked, "George, where are the children's presents?"

He put his briefcase on the table and took his shoes off. "I didn't get their presents. You have money from your piano lessons now. I thought you would buy them presents."

Mama was choking up now. "But you always get their presents."

"I never said I would get them. You just assumed that. And you assumed wrong." After making that declaration, he stomped to their bedroom and slammed the door.

With trembling fingers, Mama dialed JoAnn. When JoAnn answered, Mama struggled to get the words out: "George didn't buy the children presents. Please, can you help me?"

JoAnn and her husband, LaVelle, looked around their home for some items they could give as presents. One item they grabbed was a ukulele for me. LaVelle had a hobby of refurbishing old instruments and had just restrung this one.

Stashing a few odd gifts into her car, JoAnn drove to our house, picked up my mother, and went to a 24-hour drug store. There, they purchased suitable gifts and candy for us four kids. My mother didn't reveal how the items were paid for, but I suspect that JoAnn paid for them, too.

Four pairs of little bare feet lined up at the living room door the following day to enter our imagined fairyland. When the door was opened, we all ran to our assigned spots. I grabbed my red stocking and dumped out the candy and fruit that was stuffed inside. Then I saw the ukelele. I could hardly believe it! My girlfriend, Charlotte, had a ukulele that her dad had given her, and now I had one, too. I couldn't wait to tell Charlotte.

> **And do not forget to do good and to share with others, for with such sacrifices God is pleased.**
>
> —HEBREWS 13:16 (NIV)

I looked around the room at my siblings opening their stockings and tearing into packages of books, cars, and dolls. I thought, *we are such a blessed family. Look at all these presents!*

I scurried to the kitchen, where Daddy was reading the newspaper and drinking his coffee. "Thanks so much for everything, Daddy." I hugged him. He smiled a little and turned the page of the newspaper. Then I returned to the living room and stepped around my siblings seated on the floor to reach Mama. I threw my arms around her neck and said, "Thanks so much, Mama! Christmas is so special. You're the best!"

Leaning back, I held her face in my small hands and noticed her eyes were wet. Was Mama crying? My heart skipped a beat to think she might be unhappy on this special day.

But I breathed a sigh of relief when she whispered, "God is so good to us, isn't He?"

Calmness replaced my temporary panic. "Yes, yes, He is, Mama!"

A few weeks later, my father left a goodbye note on our kitchen table that we found when we woke up one Saturday morning. Mama took the note and read it in private, and when she came back, she served us breakfast as if nothing had changed. When she told us later that Daddy was never coming back, she reminded us that God would never leave us and that He would take care of us. Her strong faith definitely helped us accept the news. Between that and how frequently Daddy had been absent even before he moved out, we all adapted quickly.

> **Therefore, as we have opportunity, let us do good to all people, especially to those who belong to the family of believers.**
>
> —GALATIANS 6:10 (NIV)

After church the next day, the back seat of our car was full of groceries that members of the congregation had given us. While my mother was putting the food into our cupboards, I thought about how often the refrigerator was empty and why the people at church needed to give us food, and I asked her, "Mama, are we poor?" Her response still rings in my heart: "Oh no, sweetheart. We are not poor. We are rich because we have Jesus."

That summer we stayed with my grandparents in South Carolina while my mother renewed her teaching certificate.

When we returned to Georgia that fall, she found a teaching job, but even so she found it nearly impossible to make ends meet. The following year we moved to South Carolina to be near my grandparents, who helped us get on our feet financially.

After our move, God led us to a new church that was attended by friends of my mother. On our very first Sunday evening there, many cars followed us home and filled our cupboards and fridge with food! It seems that God's abundance in sending our family generous friends was not limited to Georgia.

Mama always worked hard to make sure that our needs were met, but it was the beautiful, unconditional love shown by our church family that taught me where our true treasure lay: in the love of Jesus and, by extension, the love that His children show to one another in their times of deep need.

Miracle after Miracle

Robin Ayscue

The time had come for me to try and get my life back together after having survived the most tragic events a person can endure. My only daughter, Ashley, had unexpectedly gone to heaven 18 months before. Three weeks later, my brother joined her due to Covid. Then I also lost an uncle and cousin unexpectedly, all within 5 months. It felt as though God had chosen to receive all of my immediate family in heaven and leave me here alone. But what followed showed me the power and beauty of God's love.

After each loss, I had tried to go back to work, but my job involved taking angry customer calls one right after the other, and I simply could not do it. Each time I ended up back on short-term disability. That was so very difficult for me—I had always worked and taken care of myself, and now I just could not do it. Not only did missing work cause a tremendous financial burden, but I lost faith in myself. Grief, of course, is such a powerful emotion, and to have my mind just shut down—well, it was hard.

My closest friends and family knew what was happening and were praying for me. Those prayers must have been heard, because suddenly, miracles started happening.

God placed me in the care of a wonderful counselor who understood what was happening with me. With her help, I applied for an accommodation with my employer. We requested a new schedule with different days and hours and a new work group. God gave me the perfect schedule. It made the situation better right away, and to this day it continues to help so very much. I love my new work group. If I could have picked one, it would have been the one they assigned me. Both the schedule and work group accommodation went through within a month, which was a miracle in itself—at my workplace, it usually takes months for an accommodation to be approved. God gave me the perfect agent to get the changes processed quickly. The other wonderful thing about the accommodation is that I cannot be moved from this work group or given a new schedule without my counselor's approval.

My first day back at work was April 3. The day before, two of my sweet friends, Shan and Karen, prayed a special prayer over me after church because they knew that I was so nervous about returning. I

> **The LORD is close to the brokenhearted and saves those who are crushed in spirit.**
>
> —PSALM 34:18 (NIV)

was so scared that I wouldn't be able to do it, and I truly believe that prayer helped me through.

After my first week back, my friend Shan invited me to her house for Easter Sunday lunch to celebrate with her family. That day was also my birthday, and she had a beautiful birthday cake for me. She gave me a card with a $100 bill in it! Wow!

On the way to her house, my Rusty—I will let you guess why my car's name is Rusty!—started making an awful noise and I knew I would have to bring it to a mechanic. That $100 bill sure would come in handy. I knew God had seen this trouble coming and guided Shan to give me that gift before I even knew I would need it.

I called the mechanic on Monday, and he said I could bring Rusty to him. As the Lord would have it, my always-there-for-me neighbor, Sherry, had the day off and was able to follow me to the garage, almost 20 miles away, to drop the car off and bring me home. I see God's beautiful timing in this. The end of the day brought the dreaded call from the mechanic. Rusty had several things wrong—brakes and a gas leak—and the total price would be $750. I explained that I hadn't even received my first check from work yet. He told me that I could make two payments if I needed to and that he would work with me. Plus, I could pick Rusty up on Tuesday; the mechanic would have him ready. Although I didn't know where I would get the money, it was such a blessing to me that the mechanic would let me take my car before paying.

Because I picked up the car the next day, I was able to go to Bible study at church. When it was over, our leader, Karen, gave me a card. I figured it was a late birthday card and waited until I got in my car to look at it. I settled in behind the wheel and then opened the envelope and card. To my shock, five $100 bills fell out! I ran back into the church to find Karen, only for her to say that God had told her to give it to me. *Are you kidding me?* God had done another miracle for me—but He wasn't through yet.

Before I went to bed that night, I received an email informing me that I had received a $100 payment from my counselor, Gayle. She said that she had received a big raise at work, and she asked God who she could bless, and He gave her my name. I now had received $700 surprise dollars in 3 days.

Two days later, I was going through my mail when I noticed a notecard-sized envelope. It was from a new friend named

Julie, who I had met through church and a grief sharing group. She wrote the sweetest note about how our friendship had blessed her and included $150 in cash. Not only was the money a blessing, but her sweet words meant so much to me. God had over-provided the money for the car repair in only 4 days. All of my financial blessings had added up to one big miracle!

The following Sunday, something else happened. I was headed to the kitchen to look at what I had to fix for meals for the week ahead when the doorbell rang. It was a neighbor who I would guess has been to my house 5 times in 6 years. She held two bags in her hand. "Ms. Robin, I hope this doesn't offend you, but you know, I work for US Foods and sometimes they send home food with us and, well, my freezer is full, so I thought I would bring this meat over to you. I hope you don't mind." After all the hugging and crying, I brought the bags inside. She gave me four Porterhouse steaks, ten cube steaks, and eight filet mignons! I don't have steak at my house often. Once again, God had provided!

> **How abundant are the good things that you have stored up for those who fear you, that you bestow in the sight of all, on those who take refuge in you.**
>
> —PSALM 31:19 (NIV)

On Tuesday, April 18, a pastor from my church called me. He said that he had heard I was back at work and was having some financial problems. I testified to him about the miracles that God had been doing. He said that at the church they felt like I had been through a lot for a long time, and they wanted to help lighten my burden over these last hurdles. He asked me to go gather all of my current bills and come back to the phone. He then told me that the church was going to pay every current bill that I had and that they were thankful to be able to be a blessing to me. The following Friday, all of my current bills were paid in full by the church.

A few weeks later, a neighbor that I had not seen in more than 30 years showed up at my door. She had been at the local farmers market and said the Lord told her to bring me some food. She brought me 5 pounds of organic ground beef and a dozen and a half farmers' eggs.

Then, on May 31, I was able to pay a large bill from months before that had been hanging over me. I paid the bill at lunch around 1:45. I cried as I notified those praying for me because I felt such relief. And less than 2 hours later, I received a notification that our pay stubs at work had loaded. When I opened mine and saw the amount, my mouth fell open. I couldn't believe it. It had to be a mistake. But it was not—it was my fifth-anniversary bonus of $1,500. To say that I was completely undone by His overwhelming goodness would be an understatement. I had to take time off just to cry and praise Him. In less than 2 hours, God had given me more than the bill I had just paid! A final blessing to wrap up the miraculous string of support I had received from friends, neighbors, and the church community around me.

> **He performs wonders that cannot be fathomed, miracles that cannot be counted.**
>
> —JOB 5:9 (NIV)

With blessing after blessing, miracle after miracle, working through the community of faithful around me, God had let His sweet presence be known. He proved to me that I am not alone. He is near to the brokenhearted, just as He promised.

The Hope Chest
Renee Mitchell

People don't really talk about hope chests today, but when I was growing up, young women in their late teens would get them for Christmas, birthdays and even graduation presents. A young woman was supposed to fill her hope chest with things she would need for married life, such as linens, quilts, housewares, or maybe a dress for a special occasion.

My boyfriend in high school, Larry, was an expert woodworker. He made picnic tables, bookshelves, and pretty much whatever anyone wanted. He had crafted a beautiful hope chest for another young lady in our church, and so I decided I wanted him to make me one too.

We had fun picking out the wood, handles, and even the cloth for the inside. It was a beautifully crafted piece that was made even more special because he included me in every step of the process.

In the years that followed, I set about buying things to fill up the chest. I worked after school to make extra money and had plenty of time to hunt down bargains and clearance items, so it became a hobby for me and my mom. Since I knew for certain marriage wasn't coming for quite a while, I would splurge a little every now and then to get exactly what I wanted. I was blessed as well by grandmothers, aunts, and neighbors who had heard of my new project, and it wasn't unusual for them to randomly drop by with something special for the chest. I enjoyed every moment of it!

After a few years, the chest was completely full. I began to put other items in the top of my closet, including some beautiful blankets and quilts and the most up-to-date appliances. I remember my mom commenting one day that even she didn't have some of these new things.

Then one quiet Saturday morning, the phone rang. Minutes later, my mom came running down the hallway into my bedroom. The home of a young family in our congregation had burned down that morning. The family with their three small children were OK, but they had lost everything. I stood there listening, and my heart broke. I was young, and I couldn't truly understand the impact this would have on their lives. I just knew it was a burden too great for anyone to bear alone.

> **Give, and it will be given to you. A good measure, pressed down, shaken together and running over, will be poured into your lap. For with the measure you use, it will be measured to you.**
>
> —LUKE 6:38 (NIV)

Our church didn't hesitate to jump in and help the family find a new place to stay. Eventually, after a few weeks, they were settled in their new home.

One Sunday morning soon after, our pastor announced that the family needed all kinds of home items and asked that everyone give what they could. My heart got so full I thought it would burst. I knew what I had to do. My room was full of

Beloved *by* His Faithful | 169

everything they needed, and it was all new. For one second I thought about all the time it had taken to gather those things, and remembered how often I had imagined and planned where they would go and how they would be used. But knowing this family was in such desperate need tugged at my heart. I had to trust that God would take care of me when the time came.

I went to my mom after service and told her my plan to give all of my new things to this family.

I wasn't sure she had heard me at first. She just looked at me for a minute or two, and then tears began to run down her face. She told me how proud she was of me and that she knew the Lord would bless me when I was the one starting my new home.

We went immediately and packed it all up. The family came by that afternoon to pick up what they thought was a box of used items we were donating. I will never forget the look on their faces as we brought box after box of new household appliances and other special items for them.

After everyone left, I went back into my bedroom and looked at the empty chest and closet. I knew it was the right thing to do. There was no sadness there.

The closet remained empty, though I did put a few important things I had found along the way in it. I knew it would take a lot of time and effort to replace what I had given away. Every now and then doubt and fear would try to creep in—when the time did come for me to marry, would I have what I needed?— but God would always bring peace. Though I had no idea what was to come, I knew we would always have what we needed. I turned my thoughts to everyday life and the months went by quickly.

It wasn't long before Larry proposed, and a few months after that our wedding shower came around. When I walked into that church, I couldn't believe my eyes. People were everywhere, and gifts lined the altars on both sides. Family and friends had come from all over to give us all types of household items, beautiful things. Every pew had a family in it, and there were people putting up chairs for us to sit in and surrounding us with gifts to open. One by one they handed up carefully wrapped gifts. I could hardly contain my emotion. As the evening went on, I was overwhelmed by the generosity and love that flowed from the people in the room.

When the shower ended and everyone left, we took all of those wonderful gifts to Larry's apartment, which was soon to be ours together. We found that everything I had given to that family had been given back to us five times over, including the handmade blankets and quilts! One by one, people came to me over the next few weeks and told me that they had heard about what I had done with the family that lost everything and they wanted to make sure we were blessed with what we had given away!

> **Share with the Lord's people who are in need. Practice hospitality.**
>
> —ROMANS 12:13 (NIV)

That hope chest brought joy from the time it was built until it fell apart many years later. It was used to hold blankets and children's toys and whatever I needed to put away. But no matter what I stored inside, I would always see it as the chest that held so much hope—and a sweet reminder that you can never outgive God!

Struck Down but Not Destroyed

Joanna Eccles

Bam. Bam. Bam.

Three consecutive blows knocked me off my feet in 2020.

The first hit came when my boyfriend of nearly 2 years texted me the week of Valentine's Day that he didn't think our relationship could continue. My chest tightened as tears streamed down my face. We had talked about marriage. I'd introduced him to my parents, gotten my nana's diamond appraised, and bought sparkly platform shoes to wear with a wedding gown. However, the combination of a long-distance relationship and his parents' failing health had formed cracks between us that weren't repairable.

I went to Bible study the next night to pray with a friend. While slumped against the stairwell, I accused God: "Don't You love me?" God responded that my ex was not the right man for me. In the midst of deep pain, the Lord's presence remained. Despite knowing the truth, my heart still ached.

The next shock came 2 weeks later at work when I met with my manager for routine feedback. Instead of listening to my concerns, she snarled that she wanted me gone. This blindsided me. She had started in my office a few months earlier, and I hadn't learned her expectations yet. Apparently, I wasn't meeting them. My efforts to improve my performance made things worse.

Between the stress of the relationship and work, I had three days where I barely functioned. I didn't sleep. I didn't eat. My heart thudded in my ears, and my breathing was shallow. God must have helped me drive safely into the office, because every wound in my life bled together until I couldn't see straight. My one nice colleague told me to go for a walk because I didn't look so good; I couldn't hide the pain that plagued me.

The final strike came when the world closed down for Covid-19 in mid-March. My roommate of 6 weeks left right before everything shut down to quarantine with her family. As an extrovert, I gain strength from community. Now, isolation surrounded me. My only contact outside my home was going into the office where my boss hated me.

Fabulous.

Shortly after these events converged, I sat in my car talking with a friend on the phone. I told her one advantage of hurting so deeply was that the space between myself and God had blurred. I heard the Lord clearly during that time of struggle.

She laughed. "Of course. The Lord is near the brokenhearted."

> **We are hard-pressed on every side, yet not crushed; we are perplexed, but not in despair; persecuted, but not forsaken; struck down, but not destroyed.**
>
> —2 CORINTHIANS 4:8–9 (NKJV)

Beloved *by* His Faithful | 173

My spirit resonated with her words. When we need God so desperately, His love comforts our wounded emotions and speaks soothing truths to our souls.

I attended a small church of 70 people that functioned more like a family than a Sunday morning fellowship. When the pastor learned about my turmoil, he asked the ladies in my church to send me letters. I received so many cards and coloring sheets from their children that I turned a wall of my dining room into a collage so I could see God's care for me every time I entered the room. One woman even sent a bouquet of flowers whose fragrance filled my house with a pleasant aroma and cheery colors during a dismal spring.

> **He also brought me up out of a horrible pit, out of the miry clay, and set my feet upon a rock, and established my steps.**
>
> —PSALM 40:2 (NKJV)

At work, my downward spiral continued. Working mostly from home, I went into the office every 9 working days. On the nights before I was scheduled to be there, my stomach soured and my shoulders knotted. One day, after failing to meet my boss's standards yet again, she called me into her office and gave me a harsh tongue lashing. I fought back tears of frustration as I felt inadequate once again.

Later, I asked Jesus to show me where He was during that interaction. I expected to see Jesus sitting beside me, holding my hand. Instead, God revealed Jesus standing between my boss and me, shielding me from the flames of her harsh words with His body. I wept. He took the brunt of the pain for me on one of the worst days of my life. God also helped me pray for my

GOD'S GIFT OF SIGHT
— Buck Storm —

SAN MIGUEL ISLAND is 26 miles off the coast of California. My commercial fishing boat feels small in the vast ocean as evening sets fire to the western sky.

When the sun is gone, night throws out a blanket of stars from horizon to horizon. It's a vista anyone who hasn't spent a night on the open ocean would struggle to imagine.

Believe me when I tell you that the nighttime sea-sky is a sight to wilt even the hardiest atheist.

I can't look away. It's as if the Great Artist has imagined all this only for me. Or for you.

And maybe He has.

---

boss, which changed her attitude toward me over time. She never liked me, but at least she'd greet me in the morning.

My mom took pity on me and visited in late April. She knew the risks of flying during the height of Covid-19, but couldn't bear to hear my heartache any longer. At the airport, I placed a towel in the back seat for her to sit on and sprayed her with Lysol before she entered the car. After she'd showered and changed clothes, we had a long hug. My mom's arms represented the arms of Jesus as she held me close. God never abandoned me even during those tough times.

The Lord also sent others to stay with me during those lonely days of quarantine so I didn't remain isolated. My sister visited in May for a few weeks. Then, I visited my family for a week during the Fourth of July holiday. My roommate from February returned for the month of August, and my sister moved in with me in late September. I didn't have those visits mapped out at the start of the lockdown, but God took care of me throughout that season of pain and shame.

Thankfully, seasons change. Six months after I received the poor review from my boss, I found another job. That position was much better suited to my skills. My new management routinely affirmed me and my work. God provided a place to rebuild and heal from the previous office. The Lord showed me His goodness in the land of the living and strengthened my heart as I waited on Him.

During a time when my heart could have shattered, the Lord had the final say. God's presence permeated my life. Looking back, I see how the Lord carried me through that fight. He picked me up out of a miry pit and set my feet on solid ground. God can do the same for you.

What Matters Most

Stacey Thureen

As my three kids were getting ready for their day at school, I could hear my son, Dane, telling jokes, which was very appropriate for April Fools' Day. Those jokes were being passed around the kitchen table like a plate full of good food, accompanied by laughter and smiles. It was a delightful way to start the day, but I felt the Monday morning rush catching up to me. My husband, Kyle, had already left for work. There was a little bit of fresh snow on the ground where we live in Minnesota. That meant more work on my part to make sure all three of my kids left the house with proper winter weather attire.

I was helping my youngest, Joy, get changed. She was standing by the window in the mudroom, where she would wave goodbye to her older siblings when they went to the bus stop. I squatted down and suddenly I was wracked with excruciating back pain. I knew that pain all too well. I'd thrown out my back in the same way a year ago—a year to the day, in fact. I immediately dropped to all fours, crying out to God for help while crawling my way to the family room.

"God, not again! Please help me, Jesus!" I cried out.

Meanwhile, all three of my children were looking through the mudroom door.

"Mom, are you OK?" one of them asked.

"Yes, I'll be OK. Please pray for me."

I didn't want my kids to see me in so much pain, but at least they got to see that the first words out of my mouth weren't bad words or taking God's name in vain. Rather, it was a prayer of desperation and dependence on God. I thought: *Isn't that what our Heavenly Father wants from His children? God, don't You want us to cry out to You? Don't You want our young ones to see us depend on You?*

As I got back on my feet, the pain too hard to bear, I hobbled my way into the mudroom. I kissed my oldest two goodbye, prayed for them, and gave them hugs. I assured them again that I would be OK, and off they went. I struggled to walk into the kitchen and grabbed my phone. I sent a text message to my chiropractor and scheduled to see him that evening. I also texted Kyle, asking him to pray for me.

> **"For where two or three gather in my name, there am I with them."**
>
> —MATTHEW 18:20 (NIV)

I was thankful it was still a month away from a masters swim meet I was scheduled to participate in. Based on what happened to me the year before, I knew my back would be recovered by then, and it was. But 10 days out from the competition, I developed a dry sore throat and a hoarse voice. A virus ensued that took Kyle and me out for days. It was the sickest I had been in a long time.

In that moment, I started to lose hope. That's when God showed up and instilled it right back into me, sending the believers in my life to encourage me to stay positive. Friends started contacting me through texts, emails, and phone calls checking in on me. Some got in touch completely out of the blue and had no idea what I had been going through. Others had been with me through the past year of injury and recovery, and knew how much it meant to me to stay fit and healthy so I could compete in swimming. Wayne Helm, a friend and missionary I'd met at the YMCA, prayed for me over the phone.

During this time, I learned I had much to be grateful for. It became official that an open-water swim I competed in several months prior had been awarded United States Masters Swimming All-American status. This meant that because I had won the race for my age group, I had become a national champion and honored with the title of All American. Separately, I found out that the time for the 200-meter short course butterfly I had swum a few months before was officially ranked tenth in my age group worldwide among masters swimmers! This was my first ever individual master swimming world ranking!

> **Though one may be overpowered, two can defend themselves. A cord of three strands is not quickly broken.**
>
> —ECCLESIASTES 4:12 (NIV)

I immediately called my coach, John Jacobson. "JOHN! Guess what?! I just found out my time got tenth place! I'm world-ranked!" I said with a raspy voice. I was so grateful for John's guidance and leadership over the years. Whenever I'd been injured, he helped keep me positive even though I had so many things happen that could have zapped me of hope.

But God had sent me hope in the form of all the friends who prayed for my injuries to be healed, in the form of the news about becoming a world-ranked swimmer. When the day of the next meet arrived, I had recovered enough from the virus to compete.

At the meet, I saw Wayne Helm, who prayed for me on deck. I saw many other familiar faces who asked how I was doing, who encouraged and supported me being there. The swim meet went well overall. Yes, I wanted it to be better, and I wanted to feel better in many respects, but I was glad I went. I'd learned that sometimes in life, I just need to show up and entrust the results to God.

Looking back, it was a lot to endure in one month. But there were some big blessings! And maybe the biggest were the family and faithful friends who cared about me and who blessed me with their support and prayers that helped keep me focused on Jesus.

What happened on April Fools' Day wasn't funny. The cumbersome circumstances that ensued days later weren't ideal. However, the connections with the people around me—family, friends, acquaintances—were what led up to a happy recovery. And that's what matters most.

Calming the Storm Clouds
Peggianne Wright

Ironically, the storm clouds began gathering in my life on a blazing, bright sunny Arizona morning, when our precious little Norfolk terrier, Thomas, crossed the Rainbow Bridge unexpectedly. I sat in a closet and cried for two days. Since we were not blessed with human children, my life has been devoted to taking care of our fur-kids, and Thomas in particular had been my heart dog for 14 years. Healing was slow. The only thing that helped was the fact that we still had his "sisters," a Norfolk terrier named Teegan and a rescued cockapoo named Miss Joee. The girls made living bearable, but that small cloud seemed to linger.

We returned from our winter home in Arizona to our home in Canada that fall, and a new series of dark clouds in my life began to form. My mother, who had been diagnosed with Parkinson's disease, had now developed Lewy body dementia. As Christmas arrived, we began to prepare to return to our sunny winter destination, and I was certain she wouldn't know me by the time we returned in the spring. I began praying for the Lord to take her home.

My prayers were answered just two months later when Mother lost her earthly battle. We made a frantic 2,100-mile, 44-hour journey home to a house that had been closed up for the winter. With only 2 days to prepare for Mom's funeral, it was the middle of the night when I finally had a chance to write the eulogy I was to deliver. I laid on the floor in my office praying through my sobs for the strength I needed.

The time was stressful for my entire family. Dad was crippled with overwhelming grief. Instead of supporting each other's grief and loss, old resentments surfaced, threatening to destroy an already rocky relationship with my only sibling. The next few days were devastating. Oh, how those clouds were looming.

We returned to the sunny Southwest to finish out the winter, hoping to begin the healing process. But, just a few weeks later, Teegan died in my arms as we rushed to the emergency vet, succumbing to her congestive heart disease. My heart was in a thousand pieces as I poured out my anguish to God every day. The clouds were beginning to blacken.

Just months after losing my mother, as the fall leaves began swirling in the air, my beloved dad announced to me that he had been diagnosed with bladder cancer. He assured me that he wasn't worried and said that my husband, Bill, and I should "live our lives" and go back to Arizona as planned. Before our departure, we accompanied him to his consultation and were relatively comfortable with the prognosis. A biopsy scheduled for January would be more conclusive.

On January 6, the biopsy became a near-death experience due to complications in the surgery, and by January 9, I was on a plane home to Canada from Arizona. The next day, as I held his hand, I cried with my dad. Through my tears, I asked, "Who am I going to share my faith with when you're gone?" With Mother gone, it had been only my dad and me supporting each other in faith. We prayed together that he would recover.

On his release from hospital, Dad was able to move in with my brother, and I returned to Arizona. But then our government ordered Canadians to return home due to Covid, and we left abruptly on March 19 to make our way back. We were required to quarantine for 14 days, meaning I wouldn't be allowed to visit my dad during that time. But we communicated daily by video chat, text, and phone calls until he was hospitalized again 10 days after we had arrived home.

It was Palm Sunday when the quarantine finally ended, and I was elated to know I was going to visit Dad and finally hug and kiss him. I missed him so much. He hadn't been able to communicate much over the last couple of days. But, as I stepped out of the shower, I answered my ringing phone and heard my brother's voice say, "Dad's gone. He passed away at 7:30 this morning."

Suddenly, I was engulfed with the blackest, most terrifying clouds I'd ever imagined. I felt like I was in the vortex of a tornado without hope of rescue. Without desire for rescue, really.

> **When I was in distress, I sought the LORD; at night I stretched out untiring hands, and I would not be comforted.**
>
> —PSALM 77:2 (NIV)

The next weeks were a blur as I navigated the funeral arrangements and paperwork through the restrictions of Covid. Stress, fear, anxiety, and grief. Every black cloud now had a name.

Shortly after Easter, during a Zoom call with a friend from Arizona, the subject of how we were coping with the stay-at-home requirements created by Covid came up. When my friend asked if I'd be interested in doing a Bible study with her, I enthusiastically agreed. I had never known her views on religion as we'd never spoken about anything but casual subjects like current events. So, when she expressed a desire to learn more about Jesus, I was delighted. God did that!

Over the next year, I wrote and developed a comprehensive study that took the two of us through the New Testament, one week at a time. I spent hours researching, writing, formatting, and studying so that we could grow together in the Word. But there was just one more black cloud on the horizon.

As we completed the final lesson to coincide with Easter, we had been discussing our options for our next study. Agreeing on a new topic, I eagerly began preparing. But my work came to an abrupt halt when I read her email. She no longer wanted to do the study. She had decided she wanted to do something different. She hoped I "wouldn't be upset." Just when I thought the clouds were beginning to thin, this last one, rejection, darkened my world once again.

A few days later, driving home from an errand an hour away, my brain was still crying out, *Why, why, why?* And then I thought, *What do I do now?* And God decided right there and then, enough was enough! Enough crying, enough sadness, enough self-pity. Enough clouds.

That was the moment when God began to speak to my heart, telling me that it was time to get serious about pursuing

> "Surely God is my salvation; I will trust and not be afraid. The Lord, the Lord himself, is my strength and my defense; he has become my salvation."
>
> —ISAIAH 12:2 (NIV)

the plans I had put on hold for over a year. Plans that I never had time to act on because of this study with my friend, because I had been so saturated in grief from the loss of both parents and two of my beloved fur-kids in such a short period of time. Those dark clouds were beginning to part, and I began to feel some excitement. Light broke through as I realized that this was God's plan all along.

My entire life has been devoted to the care and raising of fur-kids. Dogs in particular. My husband and I have been pet parents to a string of two cats and seven dogs over the past 43 years. My passion for all aspects of training and nurturing our pups had spilled over into an entrepreneurial endeavor of a gourmet dog-biscuit bakery, a fundraising charity walk that for the past decade focused on raising money for a local pet rescue, and now, the calling God had placed on my heart, a pet parent ministry. The clouds that had once threatened to smother me in my grief and loss have been replaced

> **You, LORD, keep my lamp burning; my God turns my darkness into light.**
>
> —PSALM 18:28 (NIV)

with the touch of the Lord's hand on my heart. He reminded me of the ways I could serve Him and become His vessel, pouring light into others' lives. Every day, my heart bursts with happiness as I interact with my website, blog, and social media followers, always striving to encourage and enlighten. Through the creativity God blessed me with, I work hard to focus on ways to bring the Word to all pet parents in the hope of edifying their daily lives and enriching their relationships with their pets in some small way.

I know my journey will undoubtedly encounter more clouds in the future; likely many of the same names as before. But, I also know that my unequivocal trust in God and His timing will always calm the storms and lead me safely into the protection of His light.

Whole Again
Tammy Gerhard

If a "double-minded man is unstable in all his ways" (James 1:8, KJV), imagine what would happen if you had forty-five different minds—forty-five different ways of thinking, feeling and behaving. This was the case for a young woman I mentor, Ann, who was diagnosed with Dissociative Identity Disorder (DID). Previously known as Multiple Personality Disorder, DID is a relatively rare diagnosis, thought to be caused by severe early childhood trauma. It is characterized by the presence of at least two distinct and enduring personality states that are accompanied by gaps in memory beyond what could be explained as normal forgetfulness.

When I was introduced to Ann, she was switching in and out of multiple personality states throughout her day, resulting in instability and chaos in her mental, personal, emotional, and spiritual life. Because of this, she was regularly in vulnerable situations. This was due to the fact that, while one "part" of her was keenly aware of a dangerous situation, another "part"—the part that was currently in control of her body—might not be. Ann would be engaging with unsafe people and finding herself physically and emotionally harmed with absolutely *no* memory of how it happened. As her mentor, it meant that I could get calls at all times of day, about all types of situations. When I answered one of her calls, I would be met with different attitudes and voice tones depending on the part that was speaking, leaving me scrambling and praying to discover who I was talking to on the other end of the line.

I met Ann when she had reached out to a national abuse hotline in the middle of a crisis and begun receiving support through a local program I was volunteering with. It wasn't long before those in charge recognized that she required more help than they were accustomed to offering. With a background in counseling and having spent many years working in mental health, trauma support, and mentoring survivors of human trafficking, I had some experience working with fragmented personalities. I was, however, located more than 1,600 miles away from where Ann lived.

I remember speaking to her on the phone that first day as I was trying to assess the situation. I could sense her desperation to have the support of someone who understood her diagnosis as well as a safe person to help unpack the trauma she had experienced. As I ended that initial call, I prayed, and I sensed very clearly that the Lord wanted me to say yes to mentoring Ann. What I didn't realize was how through my saying yes, God would show up and use me to put His love on display, challenging Ann in a way that opened her to inviting the power and person of Jesus into her story. I also didn't realize how He would change my life—and grow my faith—in the process.

One Sunday afternoon, after almost a year of mentoring calls, Ann had a major turning point. I came home from church to an angry message shouted into my phone: "Jesus doesn't work and I'm done!"

When I returned the call, Ann, still raging, screamed, "I spend every week at church, attend weekly Bible study, sing in the choir, and it doesn't even matter. *Nothing* about my life looks like what the Bible says it should, and I give up!" She went on to say that after all this time of mentoring, even more years of counseling (under the care of a licensed and experienced Christian therapist local to her) as well as being active in her church, she still felt completely disconnected from Jesus. Suddenly sounding defeated, she added, "No matter what I try, I just don't see the growth or healing I read about in the Bible or see in your life."

I quickly prayed and asked the Holy Spirit how to respond. I was aware that Ann had experienced a sizable amount of religious trauma throughout her life and understood this could color how she saw and experienced God. I felt prompted by Holy Spirit to ask her these questions: "Ann, would you consider that the Jesus I know, love, and serve, and the Jesus you say you know are not the same? And if so, would you consider inviting the *real* Jesus to come into your life and bring order out of chaos?"

> **For God is not a God of disorder but of peace.**
>
> —1 CORINTHIANS 14:33 (NIV)

I wasn't sure how she would respond. To my surprise, out of her mouth came: "Jesus, the *real* Jesus, I invite you to come into my life and bring order out of my chaos." I immediately prayed for God's help.

God answered in powerful ways. I know that is who Scripture says He is, and I believe in faith that He is able but in that moment, I don't know that I really understood what I was inviting her into or what God would teach me through it. From the moment that prayer crossed her lips, I began to notice distinct changes in Ann. She suddenly began talking about times she'd felt God's love. She laughed. I hadn't heard that from her before. Slowly but surely, I watched God do the seemingly impossible. After decades of chaotic thinking and behavior, God began to bring a structured order to the system of Ann's life.

To help me understand what was happening, she drew a map of the changes going on inside of her—a "blueprint," she called it, of what she was experiencing. In the center of her drawing was a playroom where she said Jesus would come and visit.

"Why a playroom?" I asked.

She answered, "My 'littles' need a space to play with and meet Jesus to see that He is safe." People with DID often have young parts that took on the pain of the traumatic moments the person was forced to experience during their childhood. By doing this, that part holds those memories and keeps them from the core person, allowing them to continue on with life despite the trauma. It is my belief that God allows this fragmentation as a coping mechanism to help a person being victimized survive until they reach the point of being able to invite Him into their story to bring healing.

From Ann's mouth would come words in the small voice of a child: "I'm here and I'm scared to talk to Jesus. He might hurt me." The playroom became a safe space where each part was invited to watch through a window, seeing how Jesus interacted with other parts of Ann, until they felt safe enough to meet Him themselves. Hours, days, or even weeks would pass, until eventually I would get a call and that same small voice would say, "OK, I've watched, and Jesus seems nice to the others so I'm ready to go meet Him."

Ann would later invite Jesus to set up a teen space to do the same for the older kids, then a living room for the adults. As the introductions began to take place, I got the opportunity to support each individual part as they talked with Jesus, got to know Him, and eventually invited Him into their own personal story. Then we would then begin their inner healing journey.

As I consistently prayed from afar for Ann to experience God's love, I watched Him move people into her life, including an inner healing minister local to her that specialized in working with fragmented personalities and who was excited to join our care team. God was putting Himself on display, allowing Ann to experience His love in and through a variety of people crossing her path.

I was learning a new level of God's faithfulness as He did this work. While He was teaching her that she could encounter Him directly as she prayed, He was teaching me the same thing. When something was stirring in her life and she reached out, instead of racing in to help as I might have if she lived close, I began to pray and ask the Lord to be present in the situation. I invited Him to send exactly who or what she needed and for Him to be her constant companion as she walked the situation out. Time and time again the calls came, and each time as I prayed, I would sense the direction I should take: either a call to action on my part *or* a peace to trust that He was at work in other ways. I was able to set and hold healthy boundaries and train her to use tools to connect with the Lord effectively when others weren't available.

> **Jesus looked at them and said, "With man this is impossible, but not with God; all things are possible with God."**
>
> —MARK 10:27 (NIV)

As Ann worked with her local inner healing minister, her therapist, and me, she made the decision to be baptized. The care team came together with her to celebrate.

As I flew to join the others in person for the first time, I found myself resting on the plane and experienced a vision from the Lord. A picture of a brightly colored stained-glass window came into my mind, and I sensed the Lord saying to my heart that *this* was what He was doing in Ann. He was taking each unique, individual part and melding them together into one—that in Him, she would be made *whole* again. I knew statistically it was rare for those with DID to fully integrate, but because I sensed this was from the Lord, I clung to it even in the hardest of moments. I would use it to encourage Ann when her journey to healing became increasingly difficult.

So much began to change after her baptism, but the biggest change I witnessed was that this young woman, who had experienced ongoing suicidal ideation for years, stopped making plans to take her own life. Whereas in the past, I would wake to overnight calls and texts with different parts of her in crisis and attempting to harm herself, she was beginning to learn how to invite Jesus into her hard moments, asking Him to be present and bring healing. Instead of fixating on ending her life, Jesus was at work in the core of her being and was bringing things that had been hidden in darkness for years into the light, applying His grace, truth, and love to them. Ann was learning to use the tools she had been taught by us to break agreement with the lies she had believed about herself, about God, and about others. As a result, she was discovering a reason to live and the hope that she could be healed by the God who loved her.

One by one, each different part was coming to know Jesus, giving Him their trauma. This was happening in every one of her forty-five parts—the babies and children, the teens and young adults, each individual part that held on to years of trauma and abuse was coming to meet and know the love of God in the person of Jesus. "I don't have to be afraid of Jesus. I always thought He was scary, but now I know He loves me—*all* of me," shared a once-rebellious teen part. As the team prayed and continued to walk alongside Ann, one by one each part eventually came to surrender their life to Jesus and invite Him into their story.

One day as we were talking, Ann asked about integration. Integration is the process through which the fragmented parts of a DID system come together as one whole. Until this time the parts were content with building a relationship with Jesus, seeking healing but wanting to remain as they were—independent parts. The thought of integrating had always sparked fear and anxiety in Ann, which in the past had resulted in some of her parts calling me, crying, "I like Jesus now but I still don't want to leave!" Now, as she was learning about God's love and plan for not just her healing but her wholeness, the parts of her system had begun considering what life would be like, as Ann

> **May God Himself, the God who makes everything holy and whole, make you holy and whole, put you together—spirit, soul and body—and keep you fit for the coming of our Master, Jesus Christ.**
>
> —1 THESSALONIANS 5:23 (MSG)

explained it, "living with Jesus instead of having to live in the outside world."

Over the course of the next year, integration began, and Ann became less and less chaotic as each part shared their trauma stories with Jesus and her team and then asked to go be with the Lord. Sometimes one at a time and other times in groups, Ann would take a moment to thank, bless, and release the parts that were integrating. To watch the process was awe inspiring. The result was always a sense of peace and newly acquired stability.

As this process was taking place, Ann began to find her voice in prayer. Over time, she began praying for herself, her team, and others she met, loudly and boldly, empowered by the Holy Spirit and anointed to pray for the healing and well-being of others. One of my greatest moments of joy was the first time Ann asked to pray for me. Out of her lips flowed passionate, powerful prayer, and as she held her authority in Christ, I could sense the Lord's movement in the spirit.

A few months ago, the last parts of Ann's system integrated. She was made whole by Jesus! The lengthy, involved work that began years ago culminated in a moment of complete surrender to God's will and confirmation that He was completing this work in her life. Both her inner healing minister and I were invited to be present for the sacred moment where the last parts said a final farewell, blessing and thanking one another for the important work they each had done to keep Ann safe and bring her to this point. I was in tears listening to the tender dialogue between them. They said their final goodbyes and invited Jesus to seal the transforming work He had done in Ann's life. Much like that stained-glass vision I had received less than a year prior, Ann was now whole in Christ. I was given a front-row seat to witness a miracle!

GOD'S GIFT OF TASTE
— Buck Storm —

SCIENTISTS CLAIM HUMANS have varying amounts and sizes of taste buds (which makes me wonder whose job it is to count them). It does explain the eternal mystery of why some—arguably strange—people don't think chocolate is the greatest thing in the world.

We are unique. Uniquely created and uniquely loved. God knows the number of hairs on our heads and buds on our tongue.

We experience things in ways unique to us. We all experience Jesus uniquely as well. He is truly a "personal" savior. Although He never changes, He is somehow always exactly who each of us needs Him to be.

Life continues to be challenging for Ann, but one thing is sure—God is faithful to His promises. He has affirmed, held, comforted, protected, and provided for her all throughout and continues to do so as she navigates life as a whole person. She has formally had her DID diagnosis removed from her medical records, once not thought to be a possibility. She is no longer fragmented and continues to heal and explore this new season of her journey alongside her team.

I am still amazed at how God trained and strengthened me step by step, using my life to show Ann a picture of His love in tangible ways so each of her parts could receive His greater love. I have known and walked with Jesus for almost 30 years, yet I'd never felt so sure of Him as I have in these last two, as I did what He led me to do and watched Him do things I'd only read about in Scripture. Jesus has changed and transformed not only Ann's life, but mine as well.

Last month, I flew to meet Ann and the team to support her through the process of preparing to write a book about her experience. She'd called us together because she believes God is calling her to use her story to help others facing similar struggles and give them hope. As I write Ann's story here, I realize I am doing the same. It was in the hard moments with Ann that God showed me my own brokenness, my own need for His healing touch. It was in the quiet of my prayers for this hurting young woman that Holy Spirit spoke to my heart about the places He wanted access within *me* in order to strengthen and prepare me for all He had for me to do. God knew me better than I knew myself and was aware of exactly what I needed during each moment of my day. While He was doing a work in Ann, He was also doing a work in my own life. God truly is the constant presence in our lives, our genuine hope and the only one who can bring order out of chaos and make us whole again.

We may ignore, but we can nowhere evade, the presence of God. The world is crowded with Him. He walks everywhere incognito.

—C. S. Lewis

CHAPTER 6

God Speaks through Others

An Unexpected Gift.........................200
    June Foster
A Living Miracle 205
    Christel Owoo
Postcard Presence 212
    Heather Jepsen
Minnie's Friend Jesus 216
    Leanne Jackson
A J-O-Y Ride with an Angel 219
    Roberta Messner
A Blessing and a Bright Spot...............224
    Amy Catlin Wozniak

An Unexpected Gift
June Foster

Marriage is never boring when your spouse is a soldier. Joe and I met in El Paso, Texas, and were married a year later. After spending a few years stationed at Ft. Bliss in El Paso, Joe was assigned an overseas tour in Germany. I was thrilled at the prospect of visiting Europe and making a home in this new country.

During the next 3 years, I embarked on a new chapter as an elementary teacher at the military school in Kitzingen, Germany. On weekends and school breaks, I took advantage of every opportunity to travel, exploring places like Bavaria in southern Germany, England, Switzerland, Greece, and even Norway, Sweden, and Finland.

One Christmas while we were still in Germany, Joe gave me a beautiful gold bracelet, which inspired me to start collecting charms to represent each country I visited. It was a special way to remember our overseas adventures for when we eventually returned home. In England, I chose a charm in the shape of a double-decker bus; in Greece, a replica of the Parthenon; and in Bavaria, a beer stein, among others. My bracelet gradually filled up with these cherished mementos.

Eventually, the time came to bid farewell to our home in Germany. By then, I had amassed a collection of several dozen charms, picked up a few German phrases, and soaked up the German way of life.

Back home in El Paso, my gold charm bracelet was a beloved reminder of the enchanting places we'd visited. I added my college sorority pin and my 10-year teaching recognition pin from the school district where I now worked to the bracelet. As the collection of charms continued to grow, the bracelet became a treasured symbol of a significant chapter in my life. I proudly shared the story behind each charm with anyone who asked.

A few years later, Uncle Sam decided Joe should return to Germany for another assignment. By then, I had a fulfilling job with the school district in El Paso, Texas, where we had settled into our home. Our two girls were thoroughly involved in their school, and Joe was nearing retirement. As a family, we agreed it was better for him to take the 2-year, unaccompanied tour in Germany rather than relocate the entire family for an additional 3 years of service.

At the halfway point of Joe's tour, life seemed to be moving along smoothly. The three of us were managing just fine in El Paso. So when I came home after a day of teaching one

> "Do not store up for yourselves treasures on earth, where moths and vermin destroy, and where thieves break in and steal. But store up for yourselves treasures in heaven, where moths and vermin do not destroy, and where thieves do not break in and steal."
>
> —MATTHEW 6:19–20 (NIV)

October afternoon, I could never have imagined what I was about to find.

I pressed the button to open the garage door, parked the car, and walked into the kitchen as I did every day. But this time, I froze and had to swallow hard. Drawers were open, their contents scattered across the kitchen and into the living room. Cabinet doors hung ajar, plates and cups jumbled, and several chairs were overturned. My breath caught when I noticed the empty space where the speakers for our stereo system had once sat.

I called for the girls but then realized they hadn't yet returned from school, which was a blessing. As my mind raced to make sense of what had happened, it suddenly dawned on me: we'd been robbed.

I gasped and rushed to my bedroom. The cabinet drawer where I kept my sweaters, scarves, and a few keepsakes was off its track and hanging open. I approached cautiously and found my small wooden jewelry box open and empty. I searched through the drawer and the surrounding floor, hoping to spot any pieces the thief might have overlooked. After a thorough search, my heart sank as I realized that my precious charm bracelet was gone—likely forever.

After I called 911, the local police arrived to investigate the scene. They delivered the grim news that many of these robberies were committed by drug addicts seeking items to sell for their next fix. Though it was hard to accept, I suspected my gold bracelet might have been worth enough to fund a few drug purchases. All those years spent in Germany searching for the perfect charm from different countries had seemingly amounted to nothing. *Why, Lord?* Surely, God could make sense of this.

Thankfully, my children, who are dearer to me than any bracelet, were safe when they returned from school an hour later. Still, it felt as though the thief had taken a piece of me, leaving an emptiness in my heart. I called my husband to share the news, and he later told me how helpless he felt, being so far away at his duty station on another continent.

In the weeks that followed, life continued as usual, though I mourned the loss of my bracelet every day. More than once, I recounted my tale of woe about the robbery in the teachers' lounge. My colleagues listened with patience and offered words of encouragement. Yet, the Lord spoke to me in an unexpected way through an unexpected source.

One afternoon, as I sat at my desk grading papers, the janitor came by to clean my classroom. He emptied the trash, picked up any extra debris, and swept the floors.

> "For where your treasure is, there your heart will be also."
>
> —MATTHEW 6:21 (NIV)

I looked up when he spoke to me. "Mrs. Foster, I heard about what happened to you. I'm a Christian, and I wanted to offer you some encouragement." He placed a folded piece of paper on my desk and then left the room with his bucket and broom.

I carefully unfolded the small note and began to read the words: "Do not store up for yourselves treasures on earth, where moths and vermin destroy, and where thieves break in and steal. But store up for yourselves treasures in heaven, where moths and vermin do not destroy, and where thieves do not break in and steal" (Matthew 6:19–20, NIV).

Had I been guilty of putting too much focus on my earthly treasures? I held the paper against my heart and bowed my head. "Lord, thank You for sending the school custodian to

GOD'S GIFT OF SMELL
— Kimberly Shumate —

"A WOMAN CAME to him with an alabaster jar of very expensive perfume, which she poured on his head as he was reclining at the table" (Matthew 26:7, NIV). We all have things that we value. It might be a priceless or nostalgic possession that we would never dream of parting with. It might be a valuable trinket, like expensive jewelry or a gift given to us that we could never afford ourselves. Then there are inner secrets that we hide due to shame, jealousy, or desire. When we give to God without hesitation or contemplation, the scent of our offering pours over Him, and He over us.

---

share Your Word with me. Thank You that no one can steal the most important part of my life—Your Son, Jesus."

I lifted my head and felt the burden lift. Yes, I had lost my charm bracelet, but the Lord had taken that weight upon Himself. That emptiness in my heart was filled by Jesus. I no longer needed to dwell on the loss.

The following March, I designed my spring bulletin board using verse twenty-one from the same passage the janitor had jotted down on the paper to encourage me: "For where your treasure is, there your heart will be also."

When I leave this world, I will take nothing with me, not even my bracelet, but the truth of God's Word will stay with me forever. What the janitor gave me that day will endure. I will always adore the precious gift of God's Word.

A Living Miracle
Christel Owoo

In March 2019, after the Sunday service that marked our church's 35th anniversary, two of my sisters in Christ pulled me toward the fun catwalk. Our attire, crafted from the unique fabric that had been designed for our church's anniversary, showcased a beautiful range of colors and patterns. The three of us made our way up the wooden staircase in front of the church's courtyard and gracefully walked to the side of the podium, showing off our outfits and flashing bright smiles at the cameras. I stepped down and looked around to enjoy the sizzling atmosphere—cheerful smiles, giggling girls, cozy families, and people swarming around decorated photo booths. The groovy gospel music played by the live band added the perfect touch to complete the experience.

The following morning, while joyful memories of the anniversary still lingered in my mind, I showered. As I bent down to dry my feet in our confined bathroom, the familiar routine I've followed for years, a sudden jerk of agony surged through my lower back when I tried to stand upright. I moaned in pain. In shock and confusion about what had happened, I tried to straighten up again. The intensity of the pain that followed left me paralyzed for a while, both physically and emotionally. I was stuck in an awkward squat position with one leg up. Stubborn as I am, I tried once more and let out a scream of pain.

My husband rushed into our bathroom with outstretched hands to raise me. I refused his help, terrified by the fear of the potential consequences. *I don't know how, but I'm going to do it*, I thought as I struggled to get up, groaning with even the smallest motion. As I fought through the pain, I could see the worry in my husband's eyes, his face etched with lines of concern. With both hands clenched on the sink, I mumbled in anguish, my voice trembling with fear, "I can't move; my back is locked up. I don't understand what is happening." My husband's eyes widened with worry as he wrapped his arms around my torso, his touch gentle and cautious. I can't remember the details, but somehow I ended up on the toilet seat with my upper body tilted forward.

Yesterday, I had the pleasure of walking on the catwalk during the church's anniversary festivities. Now, I feel as if I will never walk again. I thought.

With tears in my eyes, I remembered how I walked confidently on the catwalk the previous day—the contrast couldn't be any bigger. An invasion of anxious thoughts swirled through my mind like a tornado as fear squeezed my heart with an icy grip. *My spine will crumble into pieces. I'll never walk again and need a wheelchair. I'll need to stay at home forever.* I was overwhelmed, sitting there in silence, my heart pounding like crazy—I couldn't help but feel overwhelmed by the sudden turn of events. My husband was so taken aback and worried that he couldn't find the words to speak either. He dressed me and placed a chair in the bedroom, where he gently seated me. Faced with the inability to leave the house for a proper medical check-up, we resorted to a phone consult with our doctor. A muscle strain was the physician's simple diagnosis—he told us confidently that with a short two weeks of rest, I would regain my strength and be back on my feet.

The physician was wrong. After a few days I was able to move around a bit—with some help—but I was far from fully healed. Then, two weeks after my first injury, another excruciating pain hit my lower back when I made a tiny move in the evening. A phone consult with the duty doctor made it clear I needed more than rest. He told me to go to the nearest hospital even though it was night, and directed me to tell them I needed an emergency MRI scan. As the word *emergency* echoed in my mind, my heart pounded with such intensity it felt like it would explode from my chest.

Alone at home, I felt helpless. I was unable to leave the house by myself, leaving me no choice but to delay the scan until the next day.

The trip to the hospital the following morning was my first time out since the incident, and getting in and out of the car went surprisingly well. In the clinic, my husband was so concerned that he stayed with me in the MRI room, enduring the deafening noise of the machine.

> **Strengthen the feeble hands, steady the knees that give way; say to those with fearful hearts, "Be strong, do not fear; your God will come."**
>
> —ISAIAH 35:3–4 (NIV)

He collected the scan results two days later and brought home a huge envelope with scans and a small one with the written medical records. As I read the report, I felt like I was deciphering a foreign language—unfamiliar words filled every line. Google came to the rescue. My heart raced as I searched for the meaning of each medical term. The findings included ligament issues and multiple cracked and bulging disks, coupled with significant damage to my central nervous system. The weight of the diagnosis sank in, and I couldn't help but feel a knot of fear, frustration, and sadness tightening in my chest.

Another doctor's tele-consultation put me at ease, assuring me that my recovery would only take six weeks. Until then, I had to be wary of every movement and heavily rely on medication day and night. The side effects of the medicines were so intense that they left me completely drained, adding to my already overwhelming misery. The sedating effects forced me to lie down often, intensifying the agony and unease caused by the cracked disks and pinched nerves.

I counted the days in eager expectation of my healing; instead, things went downhill. Pain followed me like a shadow, clinging to my every movement like a relentless companion. Standing, lying down, walking, or sitting, each position came with its own unique array of dreadful troubles. Nerve pain presented itself in a myriad of ways—what felt like electric shocks through my legs, a sensation of daggers stabbing in my back, shooting pain, numbness, tingling, and many more. Not to mention the stiffness and loss of muscle strength. One of the worst (and strangest) experiences occurred when my feet felt like they were on fire. I depended completely on others for even the simplest tasks, like dressing myself, doing chores, or picking up things from the floor.

Frustrated, I threw in the towel after precisely six weeks, forced to admit that the promised recovery time of one and a half months was a false hope I had clung to. As I opened my eyes that morning, a deep sense of defeat consumed me—I had lost all motivation to go on. A hurricane of thoughts conquered my mind. *I have had enough. I don't want it anymore! I'm tired of being cautious and I can't stand this pain anymore. I have reached my breaking point.* The day seemed insurmountable. The weight of my heavy spirit robbed me of my smile, replacing it with an overwhelming numbness that drained every ounce of my courage to fight through. I thought it would take an eternity to recover, if I even recovered at all. Despair flooded my mind, drowning out any trace of hope or positivity.

That same morning, Stella called. We both served in the ladies' ministry at our church, where we mentored a large group of young girls. She had noticed my absence at church and felt a powerful urge to reach out and check on me that day. I explained what happened briefly, my spirit too exhausted to invest any more words into the matter. Stella became quiet. I didn't understand. Had I said anything wrong?

> **The third time he said to him, "Simon son of John, do you love me?" Peter was hurt because Jesus asked him the third time, "Do you love me?" He said, "Lord, you know all things; you know that I love you."**
>
> —JOHN 21:17 (NIV)

She cleared her throat and asked with a timid voice, "Christel, can you walk?"

"Yes," I replied.

Stella became quiet again. Then enquired for a second time, "Christel, can you walk?"

"Yes," I said cautiously, as I didn't understand why she asked me again.

Silence.

She then asked for the third time, this time with a firm voice, "Christel, you can walk?"

"Yes," I answered, now even more confused about having to respond once more.

Immediately, she exclaimed, "Christel, you are a living miracle!"

Stella narrated she knew others who had lost their mobility after the same type of injury. She highlighted one specific colleague at work who, a year earlier, stooped down to pick up his briefcase at the end of the workday, preparing to head home. At that very moment, he lost the ability to move and has been wheelchair bound ever since. Stella kept talking about the miraculous fact that I was mobile.

> **But God has surely listened and has heard my prayer.**
>
> —PSALM 66:19 (NIV)

Instantly, my perspective changed. I went from sitting in a pity puddle to praising God for His provision. Like a burst of light, my future suddenly became bright again, filling me with hope and possibilities. Instead of looking back and feeling weighed down by regret, I looked forward with renewed expectation. It hit me like a wave—I was, without a doubt, a living miracle! Gratitude and joy filled my heart, and a smile appeared on my face.

Stella's phone call became a powerful reminder of God's presence and His ability to work miracles. It shifted my perception from despair to gratitude, reminding me that even amid my pain, I was still a living testament to His love and grace. Had Stella ignored the Spirit's prompt, I would have continued to hide in the darkness of a deep hole. Instead, she obeyed God's calling and asked me thrice whether I could walk. As I pondered on this, I realized the Holy Spirit had wanted me to hear the sound of my own voice, affirming three times that I could walk—just as Peter had to affirm his love for the Lord thrice. It felt like Stella knew that my hope and positivity would be renewed with each of the three positive affirmations.

From that day on, I remained positive, focusing on every small progress and disregarding every setback, thanking God for everything. The pain didn't stop at once, nor could I suddenly burst into a joyful dance—I was still bound by limitations. But yes, I was alive, and yes, I could walk!

It would take me another three-and-a-half years to get better. However, every time I remembered that day, Stella's encouragement carried me through. Her call served as a divine intervention, giving me the hope and strength I needed to go on. Instead of dwelling on the negatives, I kept thanking God for making me a living miracle and helping me appreciate each little step forward.

Postcard Presence

Heather Jepsen

I did not grow up in the church, and I didn't experience a call to ministry until I was in my early 20s. I was living in a college town studying music when God tapped me on the shoulder and told me I had been chosen to serve. I shopped around for a church home and eventually landed at a Presbyterian church that was within walking distance of my apartment.

In the Presbyterian system, a candidate for ordained ministry is sponsored by their home church. I didn't have a childhood church that I was close to, so my college church was the one to sponsor me and say that I had a call to ministry that they would support. The Presbyterian training system is rigorous, so after graduating college I had to move several states away to attend a seminary and get my masters of divinity degree.

When I got to my new lodgings, I was surprised to find a postcard in my mailbox. It was from Ron, who was serving as the clerk at my college town church. On the postcard he said that since he was the recorder of church meetings, he thought he should also send greetings my way. *Sounds good to me*, I thought, and got busy with my schooling and my new life.

As the months went by, the postcards from Ron continued to arrive fairly regularly. At least twice a month, and sometimes more, there would be a short note in my mailbox. Nothing serious, just a word about the weather or the happenings in the church family that we shared.

When I graduated from seminary and moved to another state to begin my church service, I assumed the postcards would stop. I sent Ron a letter thanking him for the many years of kind thoughts and prayers. I was done with school, and so I thought he was done providing care for me. I could not have been more wrong.

As the years went by, the postcards from Ron continued to appear in my mailbox. Even when Ron's life changed and he moved all the way across the country for a new job, joining a new church, still the postcards came. When I got married, Ron sent a gift. When my first child was born, Ron sent books and toys. When I started working at a new church, Ron sent a stole to wear in worship. When he read a good book on ministry, Ron sent it to me. In good times and bad, greetings from Ron were always in my postbox.

> "The kingdom of heaven is like a mustard seed.... Though it is the smallest of all seeds, yet when it grows, it is the largest of garden plants and becomes a tree, so that the birds come and perch in its branches."
>
> —MATTHEW 13:31–32 (NIV)

It has now been over 20 years since I left that college town church to train to be a pastor. And for over 20 years, Ron has sent me postcards. I have heard about his kids growing up, moving to college themselves, getting married, and having their own kids. He sent a picture one Christmas of himself with a grandbaby and I hung it up in my office to remind me of my support structure. Ron tells me about his work, he tells me about his family, and he reminds me that he prays for me.

Unfortunately, I have not always been as good at staying in touch as Ron has. For his thirty-plus postcards a year, I probably send five cards in the same time span. Now that Ron is older and life circumstances have changed, his cards are more prayer requests. And those are the ones I respond to. I pray for his wife, his kids, and grandkids. I pray for him and his work. I send him greetings of comfort and joy. And I thank God for Ron's ministry, his constant presence, and support throughout my career.

> **For this reason, ever since I heard about your faith in the Lord Jesus and your love for all God's people, I have not stopped giving thanks for you, remembering you in my prayers.**
>
> —EPHESIANS 1:15–16 (NIV)

The postcard presence of my friend Ron is a reminder that not everything we do in God's name has to be a big thing. Ron's gift was very small—a postcard and a few minutes of his day spent thinking of me and saying a prayer. But all those postcards added up to form an avalanche of love and support.

Ron and I were hardly even friends when I left that first church. He was just someone I knew in passing. Now we are friends, sharing our joys and concerns together in our correspondence. We know we are there for each other, even though we have not seen each other or met in person for over two decades.

Sometimes God sends someone our way when we aren't even looking for help. Of all the people at my old church, I never would have imagined that Ron would be the one I remained in contact with years later. And I am sure when Ron started sending me postcards, he never imagined that he would keep the tradition alive for so long, following my ministry career with all its twists and turns.

The story of Ron's postcard presence inspires me as a pastor. Even small acts can make a difference in the lives of our friends and family. It reminds me of Jesus's parable of the mustard seed. Just the smallest seed—whether it's an act of faith or an act of kindness—can make the biggest difference in the world.

Ron's postcards also remind me that we never know who God might be sending our way as help. It is good to be open to all the wonderful manifestations of God's presence in our world.

The most wonderful thing about the story of Ron's postcards is that it is never too late to start this tradition yourself. We can all take a moment today to share love and support in the world around us. And perhaps we are just the person God is tapping to reach out to someone in love.

Minnie's Friend Jesus

Leanne Jackson

As a child, I looked forward to Wednesdays, when Mom went grocery shopping, and to evenings when Mom and Dad went to church meetings, so I could spend time with our babysitter, Minnie. My siblings and I played with each other until her cooking and laundry were done. Then we'd gather around our piano as Minnie played and sang her favorite hymns.

Minnie was as old as my grandmother, and I knew she loved me just as much. When she sang "Jesus Loves the Little Children," I was sure she was singing about us. I could feel that love when her warm arms wrapped tightly around my waist, her apron smelling of flour, soap, and sheets dried on the line.

Another favorite hymn of Minnie's was "I Love to Tell the Story." She sang "of unseen things above, of Jesus and His glory, of Jesus and His love." When I later learned that the author of the hymn, Katherine Hankey, was British like Minnie, it made perfect sense. Minnie was not a Sunday school teacher or missionary like Katherine; she had met her husband in England, where she was born, and then moved with him to our hometown in upstate New York. Now she rarely left her adopted hometown, but she spread Jesus's love to us just like Katherine Hankey spread the Word to others.

Minnie always began and ended her hymn singing with "What a Friend We Have in Jesus," and we would sing along with her. As we got to the line about Jesus bearing our sins and griefs, I sometimes wondered about Minnie's griefs. Mostly I wondered what it meant to be Jesus's friend.

Sometimes I got to go in the car with Mom to pick up Minnie or to drive her home. She lived in an old farmhouse surrounded by fields. Minnie told us her husband had been born in that house before 1900. I was fascinated by the well she pumped for water and the outhouse around back. I imagine she was grateful for our indoor plumbing, but she never complained.

One night, when I was ten and my sister was eight, we decided to play a prank on Minnie. I don't recall why we thought that scaring her would be fun, but we easily figured out the best time—when the house was quiet, and she was drinking tea to "settle her nerves" and pray.

After she got us all into bed, my two brothers in one bedroom, my sister and I in the other, she would put on the tea kettle. That night, we crouched at the top of the stairs, listening until we heard her relax into a chair at the kitchen table. We knew she was old, but her hearing was very good, so we crept down slowly to avoid the creaky stair.

> **Jesus said, "Let the little children come to me, and do not hinder them, for the kingdom of heaven belongs to such as these."**
>
> —MATTHEW 19:14 (NIV)

We paused at the kitchen door. Together we yelled "Boo!" then giggled as she jumped and shook.

When I saw how much we'd frightened her, I wished I could erase our prank. It wasn't as much fun as I'd thought! I braced myself for a scolding for being out of bed, especially for such a mischievous reason. But our beloved friend did not scold us; she hugged us!

I was so relieved. Minnie still loved us. Regretting our actions even more, I trudged slowly, sadly upstairs to bed.

The next day, my sister and I casually asked our parents what Minnie had told them. I was surprised when they said, "Minnie said the same thing she always does—you are wonderful children!"

> **Jesus said, "Father, forgive them, for they do not know what they are doing."**
>
> —LUKE 23:34 (NIV)

That was when I truly understood what it meant to be Jesus's friend. Minnie's love and forgiveness of us were just what her friend, Jesus, would have done. Maybe He, too, loved us children the way we are, pranks and all. I decided right then and there that I would try to live, love, and forgive like that.

Minnie was our babysitter until we moved to the other side of town when I was 14. Toward the end, we didn't need a babysitter, but we loved her and my parents knew she needed the income. A few years later, my family moved out of state, but we stayed in touch with Minnie throughout the years, sending photos and cards to keep her updated on family news.

Minnie has been in heaven for many years now, and whenever I think about her, I picture her joyously singing to "tell the old, old stories" that are her "theme in glory."

Today I'm even older than Minnie was when we played that prank, but I still think of her. I continue to sing Minnie's favorite hymns. I often wish I could tell Minnie that I love her. But I believe I show it every day, as I lovingly and imperfectly follow our friend Jesus.

A J-O-Y Ride with an Angel

Roberta Messner

It's a long way from Huntington, West Virginia, to Huntington Beach, California. But that's where I found myself, celebrating Guideposts' seventy-fifth anniversary. It was exhilarating to meet folks who had read my stories in the organization's publications for the past three decades, who cared about my story and prayed for me. I'd had many struggles along the way, including multiple surgeries and a battle with opioid addiction, and I'd always credited the love of strangers with helping me to overcome the obstacles I'd faced.

Now I was struggling once again. I'd recently had surgery to address a bone deformity. My left foot was encased in an orthopedic boot. On my right foot I wore one of the soft leather flats a cobbler had stretched to accommodate my tumors. For two decades, I'd owned the same boring style in every color and pattern. The fancy footwear I adored was the stuff of dreams. Once I fell in love with a pair of boots with a patchwork of embroidery and painted posies that I knew I could never wear. I bought them right out of a store window and turned them into a table centerpiece.

Unable to walk far on my injured left foot, I'd ended up in a wheelchair at the Guideposts gathering. Now I was headed

Beloved *by* His Faithful | 219

home, sitting alone in the hotel lobby at 4:00 a.m. with a heavy suitcase by my side, worrying about the trip ahead of me. That Los Angeles International Airport was formidable even for someone who could walk easily. How would I ever make it?

The desk clerk walked over to where I was seated and handed me an envelope with my name on it. Inside was a boldly patterned luggage tag complete with colorful, curly ribbon, a gift from a fellow Guideposts attendee who knew of the bewildering blur that might face me at baggage claim. As I snapped it onto the handle of my suitcase, a tall, smiling man in a dark suit appeared. Calvin Chung, my chauffeur for the trip to the airport.

He was a complete stranger, yet there was something instantly familiar about him. Reaching for my luggage, his eyes took in the letters on the tag I hadn't noticed at first. J-O-Y. He fairly floated to his black sedan. Once behind the wheel, he turned to face me in the back seat. "Your luggage says JOY!" he announced in a beckoning voice. "Do you know how to spell it?"

This was no spelling bee. The question took me back to the church camp of my childhood that smelled of whispering pines. A memory of something more than the woods of that wonderful campground. Something that turned the impossible into the possible. Something I'd long forgotten.

JOY!

"Why, Jesus, Others, and *You!*" I cried out. The dear, nearly forgotten summer memory took over. "*That's* the way to spell JOY!" Then I did something I would normally never have let myself do: started singing to a stranger. "I've got the joy, joy, joy, joy down in my heart..."

To my stunned amazement, Calvin answered that line the way the boys did at church camp. *"Where?"*

I shot right back with the girls' part. "Down in my heart. Down in my heart to stay!"

Calvin knew all the words, and he still lived them, even today. The joy of the Lord was the strength in his kind, sparkling eyes. As we rode along in the early morning darkness, we shared stories of the paths our lives had taken. I told him about my years as a nurse and learned that Calvin's first career had been as an accountant and auditor. His work had taken him all over the country, even to my little town of Huntington, West Virginia. Now here I was in his town, Huntington Beach, California. The world seemed so very small, and it got smaller as we talked about our faith.

Before I left his vehicle, Calvin asked if he might say a few words in a prayer for me. "Please give my new friend Roberta abundant health," he asked God. "A life of abundance. May JOY be ever hers."

> . . . for the joy of the LORD is your strength.
>
> —NEHEMIAH 8:10 (NIV)

Joy—something that's not dependent on circumstances, like happiness. It's something that survives any circumstance. Calvin spoke those words like he believed they would come true.

As I waited to board my plane, I no longer focused on my orthopedic limitations. When I arrived in Charlotte, North Carolina, for my connecting flight, I had a text from Calvin. He'd been checking on me, which solved the mystery of my waiting wheelchair and helpful attendant. He'd be praying for my safety during the rest of my journey home, too. And beyond.

An angel on this earth if there ever was one.

I never expected to hear from him again, but I did. I'd sometimes receive a text from him, wanting to see how I was doing.

Beloved *by* His Faithful | 221

"Always remember how to spell JOY!" he'd write. "Wherever life takes you. It's portable, you know. Travels anywhere." Whenever I'd hear from him, the load I carried seemed lighter. And I felt—well, joy!

But I could never be Calvin with his exuberant brand of joy, negotiating the world of airports and weary travelers with such ease. I discovered that expressions of joy are as unique as our personalities, spheres of influence, and talents. I found myself singing the joy song in my head to pass the time in doctors' waiting rooms, in line at the grocery store or at a café table, in the family waiting area at a hospital, at traffic lights, conversing with a homeless man. I'd start with the letter J. What would Jesus do here? What might JOY look like?

> **I have told you this so that my joy may be in you and that your joy may be complete.**
>
> —JOHN 15:11 (NIV)

One afternoon I took my Honda to the garage to check out a rattle. While in the waiting room, I overheard the guy at the counter mention that his wife had graduated with a degree in social work but didn't do well on standardized tests. The coming Saturday would be her third try. She knew the material, and had dreamed of working with veterans her whole life—if she could only pass that exam. *That's one of your areas, Roberta,* an Inner Voice nudged.

I reminded myself to think of what Calvin would do if he were here. I dragged my boot-encased foot to the counter. "I was a VA nurse for years," I told the guy. "I'd like to write your wife a little note about the test she's facing. I know she can do it. Our veterans need her."

GOD'S GIFT OF HEARING
— Kim Taylor Henry —

THE GIFT OF hearing permeates existence. Countless sounds fill each day. They can inform, delight, annoy, please, or protect. The ability to know when to hear and heed, and when to ignore or tune out, is critical to each person's quality of life. But there is one sound that should never be ignored: the sound of God's voice in the ears of our hearts: "Your ears will hear a voice behind you, saying, 'This is the way; walk in it'" (Isaiah 30:21, NIV). Hearing and heeding this voice will make all the difference in life.

The guy was positively astonished, the way I'd been when Calvin reached out to me. "Would you really?" he said. "That would be wonderful!"

And just like that, I was filled with something that defied that hated boot I wore. JOY! Especially when he called later to tell me his wife had aced her test.

As I lived with the fruit of God's Holy Spirit called JOY, my life began to change, and my health improved. One of the best days of all was I when I texted Calvin a photo of me wearing the boots I had bought years ago but believed I would never be able to put on, the ones that had once held jars of wildflowers on my tabletop.

"My shoes are a little over the top," I joked in the text. But the gorgeous patterns were the stuff of dreams for me, and the colorful leather fringe reminded me of the luggage tag that started it all.

The God of JOY—the one Calvin knew and lived—had transformed a vase into fancy footwear for my tumor-free feet.

A Blessing and a Bright Spot

Amy Catlin Wozniak

"Why, God? Why Debbie?" I murmured one morning as I watched the bees buzz from flower to flower. I felt disconnected from the peaceful scene. The crisp morning air and the vibrant marigolds and geraniums basking in the morning sun were a sharp contrast to my weary spirit as I hefted my 2-gallon watering can to each flower box and planter on our deck.

The flower garden, usually my sanctuary, felt different that morning as I wrestled with the questions swirling in my mind. My friend Debbie had been diagnosed with cervical cancer, and the weight of her diagnosis, along with the ongoing treatments she was facing, felt overwhelming.

The chemo had landed Debbie in the hospital, and kidney problems and dialysis added to her challenges. As a retired nurse, she took this all very well.

I didn't.

Debbie entered my life at the height of my grief after losing my stepson Ryan in a tragic accident, while she was mourning the loss of her second son. We connected through a writing group, and she quickly became a sounding board, critique partner, and friend who understood my path of sorrow. Despite her own pain from having buried three of her four children, she reached out to me, offering support and understanding. I continually asked myself how Debbie, a loving wife, mother, grandmother, and a fantastic storyteller from South Carolina, survived the kind of searing loss that comes with losing a child—not once, not twice, but three times—and kept her faith. Her remarkable strength and compassion shone through. She invited me to start an online Bible study group called Beauty for Ashes, where we welcomed women facing loss to study the Word, pray, and find community together.

The thought of her facing cancer on top of her past losses left me questioning why she had to endure yet another trial. "Why one more thing, God?" I asked as I placed the watering can in the deck box and headed into the cool of the house.

> **Praise be to the God and Father of our Lord Jesus Christ, the Father of compassion and the God of all comfort, who comforts us in all our troubles, so that we can comfort those in any trouble, with the comfort we ourselves receive from God.**
>
> —2 CORINTHIANS 1:3–4 (NIV)

If I'm honest, I battled with God about Debbie's illness. Little did I know that He was preparing an answer to my questions and sorrow.

A few weeks later, as I tended to my garden, I noticed the miniature washtub planter on my bright yellow bistro table was down to one sorry-looking stalk of the celosia I had planted.

Next to it, a weed-like plant caught my eye. It had a promising bud at its center—a pink petunia. I hadn't planted any pink petunias that summer, but, intrigued, I decided to let it grow.

Over the following weeks, the plant flourished into vibrant pink wave petunias, filling the entire pot and spilling over the sides. Their gentle fragrance in the air reminded me of Debbie, who had recently been released from the hospital. When I posted a picture on Facebook of these "volunteer" petunias, Debbie was the first to comment, saying they were an unexpected blessing from God.

Reflecting on what she said, I realized that our friendship was just that too—an unexpected blessing blooming in the midst of hardship. Debbie's faith in God was the only place where she found the comfort that soothed her deep wounds of loss. As Paul reminded the Corinthians, God's comfort doesn't stop with us; it flows through us to those who are struggling. Debbie lived out the example of 2 Corinthians 1:3–4 every day, by extending God's comfort to me and others despite her own pain. In the midst of every challenge, even her cancer, Debbie let God's love flow through her, and brought beauty and comfort to others.

July came that year, and with it, the anniversary of Ryan's death. Debbie reached out to me with the following message: "These anniversaries are tough. Just knowing that we are one heartbeat away from seeing them again helps me."

Four short months later, Debbie was reunited with her children in heaven.

I was heartbroken, with tears filling my eyes each time I saw the picture on my desktop that she had sent me during the height of her illness. Her chemo port was visible, and her strawberry-blond hair was chopped in a short cap around her head.

Despite her sickness, she had wanted me to have a piece of her, a reminder of our bond.

Just before the holiday season that year, I was scrolling through the photo gallery on my phone, looking for new pictures of our children and grandsons to print for our fireplace mantle. Suddenly, I stopped mid-scroll—there was a picture of that washtub bursting with pink petunias. I sat still for a moment, and then I couldn't help but smile, remembering what Debbie had said about them being an unexpected blessing from God. Those flowers mirrored our friendship—showing up as a surprise when I needed it most. She'd been a blessing and a bright spot during a really hard time for me. I paused for a moment and sent up a prayer of thanks to God for her and the difference she made in my life. I will never forget her.

Seven years have passed since we lost Debbie, but her legacy continues on through the flourishing Beauty for Ashes Bible study group we started together. Our group now offers love and comfort to over one hundred and thirty women in their darkest hours, just as Debbie extended her hand to me during mine. Debbie's life and friendship continue to inspire me. Her unwavering faith helped me keep reaching for my own and taught

> **And provide for those who grieve in Zion— to bestow on them a crown of beauty instead of ashes, the oil of joy instead of mourning, and a garment of praise instead of a spirit of despair.**
>
> —ISAIAH 61:3 (NIV)

me the profound power of modeling 2 Corinthians 1:3–4 by supporting others through their pain, reminding them that God is with them no matter what is happening.

Each spring, I plant vibrant hot-pink wave petunias in Debbie's memory. On her June birthday each year, I sit on my deck, savoring the delicate scent of the petunias as they warm in the sun, and sip sweet tea—my Southern best friend's drink of choice—remembering her and thanking God for the gift of her friendship on her special day.

In life's most challenging times, when grief and loss threaten to consume us, it is often through unforeseen blessings that we find renewed hope. Debbie and those surprise petunias taught me that in the tapestry of our lives, intermingled with our sorrows and losses, God weaves threads of beauty—like unexpected flowers and friendships—bright spots that remind us of His presence and help us hold on to our faith.

Contributors

Robin Ayscue   p. 162
Laura Bailey   pp. 26, 116
Mindy Baker   p. 8
Vicki Bentley   p. 150
Krystal Boelk   p. 109
Lisa Corduan   p. 66
Courtney Doyle   p. 121
Joanna Eccles   p. 172
Elizabeth Erlandson   p. 22
Constance B. Fink   p. 35
Allison Lynn Flemming   p. 42
Joe Fletcher   p. 76
June Foster   p. 200
Tammy Gerhard   p. 187
Amy Hagerup   p. 156
Lynne Hartke   p. 98
Kim Taylor Henry   pp. 91, 223
Leanne Jackson   p. 216
Heather Jepsen   pp. 12, 212
Wendy Klopfenstein   p. 132
Linda L. Kruschke   p. 120
Jenny Leavitt   p. 137
Jeanette Levellie   p. 1

Eryn Lynum   pp. 34, 78
Meadow Rue Merrill   p. 127
Roberta Messner   p. 219
Renee Mitchell   p. 168
Jennifer S. Niemann   pp. 71, 82
Christel Owoo   p. 205
Kristen Paris   pp. 16, 58
Tracy Ruckman   p. 30
Kimberly Shumate   pp. 56, 107, 204
Susan Shumway   p. 92
Buck Storm   pp. 175, 195
Jeanne Takenaka   p. 86
Stacey Thureen   p. 177
Terrie Todd   pp. 15, 155
Tina Wanamaker   p. 144
Toni L. Wilbarger   p. 49
Lawrence W. Wilson   p. 143
Rachel Wojo   p. 63
Amy Catlin Wozniak   p. 224
Peggianne Wright   p. 181
Cheryl Wyse   p. 104

Acknowledgments

Every attempt has been made to credit the sources of copyrighted material used in this book. If any such acknowledgment has been inadvertently omitted or miscredited, receipt of such information would be appreciated.

Scripture quotations marked (ESV) are taken from *The Holy Bible, English Standard Version*. Copyright © 2001 by Crossway Bibles, a division of Good News Publishers. Used by permission. All rights reserved.

Scripture quotations marked (MSG) are taken from *The Message*. Copyright © 1993, 2002, 2018 by Eugene H. Peterson.

Scripture quotations marked (NASB) are taken from the *New American Standard Bible*®, Copyright © 1960, 1971, 1977, 1995, 2020 by The Lockman Foundation. All rights reserved.

Scripture quotations marked (NIV) are taken from *The Holy Bible, New International Version*®, *NIV*®. Copyright © 1973, 1978, 1984, 2011 by Biblica, Inc. Used by permission. All rights reserved worldwide.

Scripture quotations marked (NKJV) are taken from the *New King James Version*®. Copyright © 1982 by Thomas Nelson. Used by permission. All rights reserved.

Scripture quotations marked (NLT) are taken from the *Holy Bible, New Living Translation*. Copyright © 1996, 2004, 2007, 2015 by Tyndale House Foundation. Used by permission of Tyndale House Publishers Inc., Carol Stream, Illinois. All rights reserved.

A Note from the Editors

We hope you enjoyed *Beloved by His Faithful,* published by Guideposts. For more than 75 years, Guideposts, a nonprofit organization, has been driven by a vision of a world filled with hope. We aspire to be the voice of a trusted friend, a friend who makes you feel more hopeful and connected.

By making a purchase from Guideposts, you join our community in touching millions of lives, inspiring them to believe that all things are possible through faith, hope, and prayer. Your continued support allows us to provide uplifting resources to those in need. Whether through our communities, websites, apps, or publications, we inspire our audiences, bring them together, and comfort, uplift, entertain, and guide them. Visit us at guideposts.org to learn more.

We would love to hear from you. Write us at Guideposts, P.O. Box 5815, Harlan, Iowa 51593 or call us at (800) 932-2145. Did you love *Beloved by His Faithful?* Leave a review for this product on guideposts.org/shop. Your feedback helps others in our community find relevant products.

Find inspiration, find faith, find Guideposts.
Shop our best sellers and favorites at
guideposts.org/shop
Or scan the QR code to go directly to our Shop

Printed in the United States
by Baker & Taylor Publisher Services